ACTOR'S CHOIC
Monologues for
Volume 2

ACTOR'S CHOICE:

Monologues for Women, Vol. 2

Edited by Sarah Bernstein & Erin Salvi

Playscripts Inc.

Actor's Choice: Monologues for Women, Volume 2 is published by Playscripts, Inc.
450 Seventh Avenue, Suite 809, New York, New York, 10123, www.playscripts.com

Cover design by Another Limited Rebellion

Text design and layout by Erin Salvi

First Edition: October 2013

10 9 8 7 6 5 4 3 2 1

Editor's Note: In some of the monologues in this book, dialogue or stage directions from the play may have been removed for clarity's sake.

Library of Congress Cataloging-in-Publication Data

Actor's choice: monologues for women / edited by Erin Detrick.
p. cm.
Summary: "Collection of monologues from the Playscripts, Inc. catalog of plays, representing a variety of American playwrights. The source material for each monologue may be found on the Playscripts website, where nearly the entire text of every play can be read for free. Intended for female actors"--Provided by publisher.
ISBN-13: 978-0-9709046-4-5 (pbk.)
Volume 2 ISBN-13: 978-1-62384-001-3 (pbk.)
1. Monologues. 2. Acting. 3. American drama--20th century. 4. Women--Drama. I. Detrick, Erin, 1981-
PN2080.A2873 2008
808.82'45--dc22

2007050161

Acknowledgments

First and foremost, this book was made possible by all of the exceptionally talented playwrights who so generously allowed us to include their work. We are deeply appreciative.

Special thanks are due to Davis Alianiello, Brittanie Black, Brendan Conheady, Cate Fricke, Lizi Latimer, Kate Mulley, Jason Pizzarello, Noah Scalin, and Rachael Small for their monumental contributions to the creation of this book.

TABLE OF CONTENTS

COMEDY

DRAMA

INTRODUCTION

Finding the perfect monologue can be a complicated task. You need a strong, juicy piece of material that will highlight your talents—preferably a piece that hasn't been seen thousands of times already. Furthermore, to fully understand the context of your monologue, you need the play itself at your fingertips to help you prepare. Often that play is impossible to track down. That's where *Actor's Choice* comes in.

We now publish over 1,800 titles, many of which had not even been written when the initial *Actor's Choice* monologue collections were released. There's a wealth of engaging, dynamic monologues found within these new plays—and we're thrilled to make many of them available to you in this book.

But here's what makes *Actor's Choice* truly unique: For every monologue, you have the option of reading up to 90% of the play it comes from, all from one source, and all for free. Simply visit the Playscripts, Inc. website at *www.playscripts.com*. No longer do you have to waste time searching for a script—the work's already done for you.

On behalf of all the exceptional playwrights represented in this book, we hope that you enjoy these monologues, and that you get the part!

HOW TO USE THIS BOOK

Every monologue in this book is preceded by a brief description that introduces the context. If you'd like to read the play itself, we've made the process simple:

- Go to the Playscripts, Inc. website: *www.playscripts.com.*
- Run a search for the play title.
- Click the *Free Sample* link and read away.
- If you'd like to read the entire play, you may order a book at any time from the Playscripts, Inc. website.
- Note that some of the monologues have been stitched together to make sense out of context. A bracketed ellipsis [...] indicates that lines of dialogue or stage directions have been cut. In some cases, we were asked to retain all characters and dialogue within a scene; in these cases, we have indented this material and set it within brackets.

FOREWORD

"Monologue" is a potent word. It carries history. It also holds stigma. Not surprisingly, those three syllables trigger an immediate response in actors. Most often, what comes up are feelings of dread, pressure, isolation, and judgment. "It's not a natural part of acting," a young actor might say, "I wish I had someone to act with." Or, "We shouldn't be made to do these. It feels like a test."

I must confess that I have felt all the above. I remember right out of Drama School, at 22, telling my first agent, "I won't go to any audition that requires a monologue." I relay this not out of pride in my youthful presumptuousness, but rather, as an example of my fear. Clearly, even at that age, my fear of monologues had hardened into judgment.

How did this happen? Where did we get the notion that monologues are not a part of acting? When did we start burdening ourselves with the outsized expectations of "succeeding" and "nailing it" so that monologues were made to feel like such heavy lifting? Somewhere, somehow, we have separated ourselves from the essence of storytelling, the act of being in dialogue with another, in collaboration with a playwright. We've turned this "wall of words" into a mere test to get a job, something to "get right," a way to entertain and impress, rather than an exquisite opportunity to illuminate the truth. We've forgotten the beauty of why they exist.

I would love to shift the reputation of "The Monologue."

E.M. Forster writes in the opening line of *Howards End*: "Only connect." Yet, in performing a monologue, this is a challenge, as we find ourselves standing alone on a bare stage, or in a strange room, saying, "Look at me here alone. I'll try to be as interesting as I can." To what do we connect standing there by ourselves? How can we feel we are in the center of an artistic experience?

One way to begin is to look at the origin of the word. Taken from the Ancient Greek "monologos," "speaking alone," or "solo word." But "logos" also means "A divine utterance; a divine wisdom manifest in words." In this meaning, I think, is an opportunity to open the door to pleasure, purpose, and imagination. That is why the playwright wrote us that wall of words, and that can be the actor's glorious and potent undertaking: to manifest, through words, the divine struggle to be human.

The monologue is often the richest key to character in a play. It is the character at his/her most private, sharing thoughts that are heightened, personal, and often gorgeously articulate. And it can be acting at its most challenging as the actor endeavors to hold the attention of "the groundlings" and to lift them beyond their own imaginings, bringing them a little closer to knowing themselves.

As Head of Acting at NYU's Graduate Acting Program I audition over 800 students a year. As each actor brings in two contrasting monologues, that means I see over 1,600 monologues performed every year over a three-month period. It's a fascinating and at times exhausting experience. Not because it's hard to listen to that number of monologues, but because it's hard to listen to so many bad ones. I'm a very willing audience member. I yearn to see human behavior I recognize and I yearn to see human behavior unfamiliar to me, so that I might gain a bit of wisdom about others who aren't in my sphere. I can see the same monologue done eight times in a row and I'll say to myself "I never want to hear that monologue again." Then, the next actor will walk in and do that same monologue in a way that's so fresh that all those other eight versions fall away. I'm a child again in the room, hearing it for the first time. What's the difference? And why does it seem to happen so rarely?

When I began auditioning for our program back in 1998, it often seemed that there was an explosion of individuality in the room. The points of view taken in monologues, while not always necessarily good, were certainly courageous. Idiosyncratic. It seemed the actor was saying "Look at how I see this character. This is my interpretation and I stand behind it" with unwavering accountability. The bad were bold and the good were bolder.

These days actors seem more tame walking into the room. It's unusual to see someone come in with a strong opinion or a passion for what they're saying. The size of their truth seems small, about the size of an iPhone screen; more polite than courageous. It's as if the actor is so concerned with being "real," that their work comes off as generic, safe and unimportant. They offer us a gentle experience rather than a necessary one. Their truthfulness lacks appetite; it lacks the need to communicate a desire, to express something personal and deep, something razor-smart and challenging. To be inside a moment that changes the course of that character's life. These moments in time "radiate" inside us, as Michael Chekhov says. Otherwise, why do we need to say it out loud?

Here's some advice: Don't mistake comfort for truth. Don't fall into a pattern of predictability or sameness just to feel safe. Go out on the skinny branches and dare to fall. Make mistakes in front us. Be impulsive. Stumble with pride. We'll love seeing the search much more than the answer. Reinvest your sense of truth and expectation each time you say those words. Dare to be wrong. I'd rather see a moment be alive in a wrong choice than dull in a safe one. As Hamlet says, "The readiness is all."

Love your monologue. Love your character's ability to articulate so beautifully. Love them in their desire to reach for the divine. And love your author. He/she needs you to be a vessel, a grand interpreter, to give over to the written words, and to help reveal the human condition. Do the digging and then lift off into the monologue that can become a soliloquy, an aria, a portrait, a movement, a dance. Now that is something to celebrate.

–Janet Zarish

Head of Acting,
NYU Tisch School of the Arts
Graduate Acting Program

COMEDY

ACT A LADY

Jordan Harrison

Dorothy is a stern and high-minded accordion teacher in Prohibition-era America. She reflects on her craft and her town's upcoming theater production, where the men plan to dress in "fancy-type, women-type clothes."

DOROTHY. Gotta have fleet fleet fingers for playing the accordion with. I tell my students maybe you can *play* with little shorty fingers but you can't never be truly great. Better to kick a football with fingers like that, little Jimmy, little Suzie. Maybe one in every thirty of them gonna make something o' themselves on the accordion. Sometimes they take it hard, but I know I'm saving them more hard down the road.

(She wiggles her fingers: looking at them, their power.)

Pa started me early. Right outta the crib, so the weight feels just *right.* And with my fingers on the keys, it's like I've got eighty fingers rather than eight, blacks and whites, shiny.

[(She plays a nimble little riff, up and down the scale.)]

I know eighteen songs by heart and I can fake at least forty if you hum along to help me off. Here's one I wrote. Naturally, this is one I know by heart. *([She plays us a song,] Singing:)*

it's a high high time when i got time to lose
it's a high time when i wear my high shiny shoes
wear my high shiny shoes for stepping on
the bad bad devilman's toes.

That's the start to one I wrote. I like how it's a surprise at the end of the line. Thinking this is just a night for dancing in fancy shoes but really it's for stomping out sin. To me that's art. When you think you know how to see something but when you're done you see it someway else. Now tell me what's art about a gent in a dress, that's all I'm asking.

I mean to play in their fancy freakshow and I mean to play my best. I'll play until Miles comes crawling back to me, touches me on both knees and wrinkles my stockings, looks up at me, puppy-dog face, and says "Dottie I was wrong. I been making myself the fool, Dot, you were right all along." And I'll say no, Miles honey, you got bit by the vaudeville bug and you *shined* in fronta those footlights, Miles you shined like a star you could never play the fool. But I'll be smiling inside, ear to car, and isn't that the best kinda winning?

ACT A LADY

Jordan Harrison

A small, Midwest theater company has hired Zina—a severe-looking, cosmopolitan director—to helm their production. She addresses the cast for the first time, preparing the ragtag group of men for their impending stage roles as elegant, aristocratic ladies.

ZINA. *(Mit sturm und drang:)* The tale of a headstrong woman torn between love and society, keenly aware of the commerce of her own body, with the French Revolution as its backdrop!

The sad-eyed Mathilde St. Roquefort. The elegant Mathilde who must kill for love. Has any of *you* ever killed for love? *(Pause.)* Has anyone ever been in love? Raise your hand if you've ever been in love. *(Pause.)* Okay raise your hand if you ever *liked* someone a whole awful lot. Good, good.

The story of the Countess Roquefort is an old and tragic one, and—in a sparkling new adaptation by me—we intend to do it justice. Maeterlinck failed, Meyerhold failed, the great and noble Mistletwerpe failed miserably but we
will
not
fail.

(She reigns herself in.) It won't be easy. Three *weeks* of rehearsal: Not how we prefer to work on the continent. But in this mere fortnight and a half, you will submit to an exacting regimen of Dell Sarte technique, gymnastics… *(Perhaps she performs a rather lumbering cartwheel.)* …trampolining, music appreciation, and of course, the modern dance. *(She strikes an oblique Isadora Duncan-like pose.)* …until every one of you are flawless specimens of stage beauty.

Why have so many attempted this classic tale of becoming? One-hundred years before Nora gave up her macaroons, the Countess left the comforts of her own *modus vivendi*. Many have found that the story wakes them from their own drawing rooms, out into the sunlight of self-awareness. *(Fierce:)* Are you brave enough to let it wake you? I could use some coffee. Someone was getting my coffee. Where's the girl with my coffee?

All I Really Need to Know I Learned from Being a Zombie

Jason Pizzarello

A young woman enters, limping. Her left arm is missing a hand (at least). There's a bandage around her head covering up a missing eye and an ear. She's damaged goods, even for a zombie. Around her neck hangs a dirty cloth bag covered in dried blood stains.

YOUNG ZOMBIE WOMAN. Fourteen.
That was my age when I…
turned.
That was six years ago. So
Now I'm twenty.
I guess.
Not that I've aged in a normal, alive-sort-of-way.
Two thousand one hundred and seventy-eight days.
That's a little over six years.
Six plus fourteen equals twenty.
Right?
Zombies aren't known for their math skills,
But I've always loved numbers.
They're complete in themselves,
But fit neatly together with others.
And when you add them up,
they're more than the sum of their parts.
I'd like to think of myself the same way.
That I'm more than the sum of my parts.
Some days I feel like I'm falling to pieces.
And then I remember that I literally am.
Falling to pieces.
That makes me laugh
most days.

(She takes the bag off from around her neck and opens it up.)

I keep the pieces that fall off in here.
Let's see what we've got.

(She takes a couple of fingers.)

A couple of fingers. Those never stay on.
Here's a toe. Which one is it?
One of the middle ones.

(She takes out an ear.)

Aw. My ear.
I remember when that came off. It's actually a funny story.
Funny if you're a zombie.
But you probably wouldn't get it.

(She shakes the bag and looks in.)

There's a bunch of stuff in there.

(She puts the pieces back in the bag.
She closes it and hangs it back around her neck.
She takes a moment and looks at her body.)

Don't have many pieces left, actually.
But I'm thankful I haven't lost them.
I call the remaining pieces I do have, "blessings."
And I count them every night.

(She points to different body parts.)

One…
Two…
Three…
Four…
Five…

(Then to her teeth:)

Six, seven, eight, nine, ten.

(She smiles with everything she has left.)

CHILDREN AT PLAY

Jordan Seavey

Five friends in Brooklyn barely make it through junior high, only to be given this speech by their new principal on their first day of high school.

PRINCIPAL MANN. Good morning!

(Pause.)

I said, GOOD MORNING!

[(There's a weak "Good morning" back.)]

Lovely. My name is Principal Mann and I'll be your principal for the next four years...hopefully...and I'm going to let you kids in on a little secret. The Secret of Success. To succeed as a student at...what is this...? Oh, right, "Martin Luther King Junior High School"...

[(Giggles from her audience.)]

I don't...OH! Martin Luther King, Jr. High School. Hey, let me tell you something. You go from school to school to school to school, and after a while, you're like, Where the hell am I?

(A long, deep sigh.)

The Secret of Success. To succeed, here's what you have to do: just... show...up. Just drag your sweet little mugs to school. But don't bring box cutters when you do.

Hey. Don't bring guns to school. Or knives. Or box cutters. Weapons, as a general rule, are out.

Drugs: If you do 'em, great. Just don't do 'em here. Alcohol: Well... honestly? Go ahead and drink.

Don't have babies. Don't have abortions. Don't get pregnant and then try to cut it out with a box cutter.

Leave gambling till after the last school bell—or take it the OTB. No human trafficking on school premises. Anymore. Seriously. And I know how slippery teenage boys' hands get around their pretty young English teacher's ta-ta's.

Which is a good segue to my last three points:

One. Student-teacher relationships. They are strictly, expressly, prodigiously, exaggeratedly forbidden.

Two. Setting the library on fire. Do NOT do that again.

And three. Suicide. We had a student hang themselves from a hallway light fixture last year. *No more of that.*

That said...welcome to high school!

CURRENT ECONOMIC CONDITIONS

Don Zolidis

26-year-old Lily is newly unemployed, forcing her to move back in with her parents. Desperate to find work, she applies for any and every job listing she can find, only to find herself in the middle of an interview with the CIA. It isn't going well.

LILY. Okay. Hi. I'm actually a really great employee. I think I have a sparkling wit and that helps lighten things up in the office and maybe you could use that since you're trying to save the country and topple foreign governments and everything—but please, actually. I would really love to have this job. I would. I've been unemployed for about five months now and I know that's really not all that much but trust me, I am *sick* of being unemployed, I want to have a job really really bad and I would do such a great job for you guys, I would like surrender my entire life to the job, you'd come to work, and all the research would be done and everything—like, whatever you want, you want coffee, you want me to go to Morocco and get coffee, you want me to go to Morocco and release a super-virus that destroys coffee trees, I would do it, no questions asked, I don't really have any ethics here guys, I would do anything. Seriously. And if you like, wanted me to be a deep undercover spy or something I would do that too, I think I could work out a lot and look really great in a leather suit or something, not that you guys wear leather suits, but whatever the uniform is, I'd wear it. Please. Please hire me.

DEAR HARVEY

Patricia Loughrey

Jackie Grover was interviewed by the playwright in Long Beach Ca. in 2008. In her late 60s she was still an active member of OLOC (Old Lesbians Organizing for Change). Jackie is strong, determined, and direct. Life's storms have not defeated her spirit of hope and her can-do attitude.

JACKIE GROVER. I think it was Ivy Bottini who concocted the idea, because a Gallup Poll had come out, showing that people were less like likely to vote away our rights if they had actually met one: met an actual gay or lesbian person.

So we hired a bus, and got a bunch of us women—you hear a lot about what the men did but women were right up there too, organizing: Ivy Bottini, Pat Bond, Sally Gearhart—

…so, a bunch of us from the Golden Gate Chapter got into what I call "little-lady clothes:"

little skirts, matching purse, heels and hose—we were told to look as straight as possible—and took this bus to the San Joaquin Valley. They would drop three of us off at a supermarket, and then move on to the next town. Modesto, Merced, Fresno, Visalia, Porterville: all down the valley. We were met by the local chapter women from NOW who'd bring card tables and chairs. We had information and we put it on the table with a little sign out there saying, "Meet your Local Lesbian." And so we looked like Joe Schmoe from Kokomo, you know we looked like anybody else. We were there to answer questions, meet and greet, and then the bus would come back and pick us up and take us home. Back to San Francisco. There was a lot of being made fun of at first, but we learned to smile and say: "If you've got any questions we'd be happy to answer them." And we didn't look "arrrggg" menacing or anything. It was just a matter of getting so they could see we didn't have horns.

THE DIARIES OF ADAM AND EVE

adapted by Ron Fitzgerald

FROM THE STORY BY MARK TWAIN

Eve, an inquisitive woman, reflects on her relationship with Adam after their expulsion from the Garden.

EVE. When I look back, the Garden is a dream to me. It was beautiful, surpassingly beautiful, enchantingly beautiful. And now it is lost.

The Garden is lost, but I have found Adam. Which is something. I guess. He loves me as well as he can. And I love him with all the strength of my heart.

But why do I love him? I don't know.

I love certain birds because of their song. But I don't love Adam on account of his singing. Oh no, it's not that. The more he sings the more I wish he'd stop. But I ask him to sing anyway, because I want to learn to like everything he's interested in. I'm sure I can learn because at first I couldn't stand his singing. But now I can. Almost. It sours the milk, but it doesn't matter. I can get used to that kind of milk.

It's not on account of his intelligence that I love him. Oh no, it's not that. He's not to blame for his intelligence. Such as it is. He's self-educated, and does really know a bunch of things. Of course they're mostly wrong…

It's not on account of his hard work that I love him. No, it's not that. I think he has it in him. Somewhere. Though I don't know where.

Then why is it that I love him? Merely because he is masculine, I think.

At bottom he's good. And I love him for that. He is strong and handsome, and I love him for that. And I admire him and am proud of him. But I could love him without these things. If he were plain, I'd still love him. If he were a wreck, I'd still love him.

I think I love him merely because he's mine and he's masculine. There is no other reason. Love is not a product of logic and statistics. It just comes. Love can't explain itself. And Love doesn't need to.

(She yells offstage.)

Cain! Cain! You get that out of your mouth this instant. I don't care what the parrot said, you put that down.

THE DOG LOGS

CJ Johnson

Pepper is a three-year-old female Chihuahua.

PEPPER. Oh my God. Can you believe it? Trixie is not speaking to Belacourte. *Again.* Like, it was only a month ago or so they made up. And now it's the silent treatment—again. And when Trixie gets silent she gets all the way silent.

You wanna know what happened? Oh my God! It was soooooo intense! And it had nothing to do with last week. It was *totally* Bela's fault. I think.

I mean, Bela had no business being such a *bitch* at that party. I mean, did she? It wasn't Trixie's fault that she arrived in a car of her own. That's what she gets now. That's what she *deserves* now. That Bela, she can be such a bitch.

Not that Trixie can't be a bitch. She can be a full-scale *bitch!* Like, at my mistress's premiere the other day, when we were walking the red carpet, Trixie and her mistress and me and mine, well, Trixie just went so *cute-OTT* that *OMG she* got in all the papers! And it was *my mistress's movie!* My mistress cried about that. God that Trixie can be a bitch.

But anyway, who cares about any of this—I gotta tell you about this hunky bull I've been noticing out the front of Luis Vuitton on Rodeo Drive. He's *sooo* hot! He's *ripped* and he's got a gold collar—he's *bad,* you know? Like, *totally bad ass.*

And I think he's noticed me! But he's playing it cool. Because, well, you *know* he's *totally* bad-ass…I think he might be from the *streets.*

That bitch Trixie…if she saw me with him, that'd show her.

EXIT, PURSUED BY A BEAR

Lauren Gunderson

Nan Carter is a sweet southern woman attempting to break free of an abusive marriage through radical means—tying her husband to a chair, re-enacting scenes of his abuse for him, leaving him and then letting the wild bears finish him off. But she doesn't want you to think she's a bad person.

NAN. I thought you might be trying to figure out whose side you're on.

I'm not a violent person. But it's like when you get a project in your head—like an herb garden or buying new scissors—and you just can't focus till it's done? Well I just cannot rest until this's done. "This" means Kyle, and "done" means…"bear"?

God. See, that sounds awful. I don't mean it that way. I'm just…I'm—ok. Here's what I am.

I am Nan Carter. I grew up here. I loved my parents. I went to church. I married a man I thought was gonna be good. He wasn't. And my big decisions kinda stopped there. And I've seen *Thelma and Louise* so I get that I have a choice in my future; but I never felt like I could drive a Thunderbird into a canyon.

I'm one of those women that you look at and think, "Why doesn't she just leave?" Well I didn't leave until now because I'm broke, and I'm stuck, and I'm scared. I am scared.

I am Nan Carter. And I wish Jimmy Carter was my dad but he's not.

I am Nan Carter. And I wish someone had told me to wait to settle down, and to not be so sweet, and to move to Atlanta after school, and to seriously consider professional soccer—y'all I was good—and to not marry the first one, and to master the art of sedition, and to listen to my mom, and to cook healthier but Kyle doesn't like salads, like *any* salads *goddammit.*

And he wasn't always so angry, but he is angry all the time now. And he has never asked me what I want to eat. And he is awful and I wish he was dead—oh my god please forgive me but I wish he was dead. I wish he was secretly rich and then dead.

I am Nan Carter and I am alive in this wide world.

So I will be leaving tonight for good.

EXIT, PURSUED BY A BEAR

Lauren Gunderson

Sweetheart is the ultimate southern sidekick. This wannabe actress will do anything to help her friend finally leave her abusive husband, including introducing her to Shakespeare.

SWEETHEART. Here's my deal, y'all.

Two months ago I was on my way to audition for *Hamlet* at the Dahlonega Community Players when I first saw Nan. She was at the Subway just tearing through this foot long with all that stringy lettuce and crying and mauling those poor SunChips.

And I thought—this is real drama. Investigate.

So I asked her if she needed anything. And she told me that she didn't believe in love or justice anymore.

And I was like: whoa. Deep drama, y'all.

So I told her I was going to this audition—cause *Hamlet*'s got some major justice, kids. And she went with me, and then we got some food at the Chick-Fil-A, and it was over those super puffy waffle fries that we became friends. I told her about my dreams of acting (I did not get the role of Hamlet, however), and she told me about her dream of saving animals (she works at this small vet in Canton), and I gave her my copy of *The Collected Works of William Shakespeare,* and she gave me free cat check-ups.

I even told her I was stripping at the Highway Club until I got my big break. And she didn't hate me for it. Which some people do.

And after a month of sharing books and meals and funny LOL cat pictures—she told me about Kyle and love and justice and how there was a bigger truth at stake if only she had the courage. And I said…

Let's get classical.

FAT KIDS ON FIRE

Bekah Brunstetter

Nurse Joy is the highly committed head counselor of New Image Camp Vanguard. She interrogates Bridger, a quiet and allegedly dangerous camper.

NURSE JOY. I'm just curious. If I wanted to build a bomb, how would I do it? Just curious. Bored, I guess.

(BRIDGER *is silent.)*

The girl campers of Dorm West said they saw you leering outside their window at 2 a.m. They feel like they are in danger. We have this problem with you every year, and I know your parents find it appropriate to keep dumping you here because they can't think of anything better to do with you, but I do *not* deal with behavioral problems. I have enough on my plate and I am trying to run a tight ship. DO NOT FUTZ WITH MY BOAT!

(BRIDGER *doesn't respond.)*

I think you're faking it. I think you're bored. I think that you think you're Sylvia Plath. I think you need a tan. Like Mark. *(Pause.)* Mark thinks so too.

*[(*MARK *nods.)]*

All I'm saying is that it wouldn't kill you to strive towards some sort— of social life. Use words. Find a lady friend. Mark thinks so too.

*[(*MARK *nods.)]*

Anything?

(BRIDGER *is silent.)*

You and I are both getting too old for this. Just tell me I don't need to worry. Tell me I don't need to call your Dad.

(BRIDGER *is silent.)*

Well, I'm glad we had this chat. Go on now and bite the heads off pigeons or leer or whatever it is that you—do.

HAIL MARY!

Tom Dudzick

Mary Wytkowski is a young unconventional novice and teacher's assistant in a Catholic elementary school. Here she is being put on the spot by her strict Mother Superior, who wonders what possessed Mary to consider the sisterhood at all.

MARY. Well, no, I didn't hear a voice. I, um…well, okay, I did hear a voice. Mine. It was during college. I was sitting in class and the teacher was going around asking us, one by one, what our plans were for after graduation. And I was clueless. All these kids were so sure of their futures. Some of them already had jobs lined up in big banks and things. And here I'm thinking, "Well…there's this ketchup factory down the road. I could try the bottling department. They probably have a pension plan." Then the teacher was getting closer and I was getting really upset because I didn't want to be the only dummy. And he says, "So, Mary, how about you?" And I said—

(Casually:)

"I'm going to be a nun." …I was the most surprised one in the room. I have no idea where that came from! I had never considered the religious life. Never, not once. What made me say it? Then I couldn't get it out of my head. It was like the words took on a power of their own. I tried to resist, believe me. I'd say, "No, no, I want to be normal. I want to go on horrible blind dates! I want to work in an office and get drunk at the Christmas party! Throw up on my boss!" But after graduation, guess where I got a job. Teaching kids in a Catholic school. And I liked it! But still it wasn't enough. I could still hear those words in my head, "I'm going to be a nun." Finally I just surrendered because I realized, of course—*God* put those words there.

(Shrugs.)

And here I am.

HEDDATRON

Elizabeth Meriwether

Nugget, an extremely precocious ten-year-old, gives a fairly unusual report on Hedda Gabler.

NUGGET. The summer of 1890 was a wretched summer. It was wretched. So why was the great theater masterpiece *Hedda Gabler* written? No one really knows.

[...]

But, after he wrote it, everyone hated it. They said, quote: "We neither understand nor believe in Hedda Gabler. She is not related to anyone we know." And then later the people who wrote papers said: quote, "Hedda is a 'study in a vacuum,'" which is stupid, because it's not, it's in a living room. Wow. These people are really angry.

[...]

I was angry when my mom tried to kill herself and then she was abducted by robots and forced to perform *Hedda Gabler.* But then my mom came back. And every day I think maybe one day she's going to kill herself again but sometimes we perform scenes from this play, and it's okay. So you can't just say that the play is cold and impersonal, because how do you know? Maybe the day you saw it was just a bad day. Maybe you're a stupid person. I don't know why Ibsen wrote *Hedda Gabler.* But maybe that's the point. Hedda doesn't want to be understood; she doesn't want us to say, "Oh, that play was so well-made." It's like it got out of control. It's like Ibsen just let it break itself. Why did he build something just so it could destroy itself from the inside?

(A slight pause.)

If you're a robot and you figure out you're a robot—are you still a robot? Who do you become?

(A slight pause.)

I don't know. Also I brought blow-pops.

THE INTERNATIONALIST

Anne Washburn

Irene tells a story of misplaced courage and mistaken identity. Although Irene is not American, she does not speak with a discernable accent.

IRENE. One night, it's late, we're both asleep—my boyfriend and I—we're both asleep in our bed, and we hear this, terrible noise, in the garden. And at first I think—because I'm just awake you know—I think that it is a baby and that someone is killing it in the garden. And so I run to the window and I look out and there is some moonlight and I see in the shadows that a fox has my kitty—I had at the time a speckled kitty, it had a terrible temperament but I had a great affection for it and the fox has it and is trying to drag it away but the kitty is putting up a tremendous fight. And so my boyfriend and I we bolt out—and we sleep in the nude you know and we don't stop, to put on *anything*—and we run out into the garden and there's our cat, fighting furiously with a fox and there's all of this screaming and I don't know what I was thinking because I'm not brave but I ran straight at them and I grabbed—I grabbed the kitty from behind and I tugged. And the fox is holding on to the cat for dear life and I'm tugging at the cat and the fox is tugging at the cat and my boyfriend I think he's literally jumping up and down and he's yelling something and I'm tugging and the fox is tugging and then all of the sudden the cat comes loose into my hands and I just I look down and I realize, that I'm holding, a narmont!

(Laughter.)

[...] So the narmont is looking at me, and it is completely astonished, and the fox is looking at me and it's astonished. And then the narmont looks at the fox and the fox looks at the narmont and then they both look at me, at the naked human. Everyone is looking at everyone else. It's a very surreal moment.

And by this time the neighbors are awake and I see them in their windows, they're looking at me and my boyfriend hopping around naked in the moonlight with a fox and a narmont.

(Laughter.)

Their faces! I wish I could have a picture. We go back into the apartment and the cat is fast asleep in a chair on the balcony. Fast asleep. I wanted to give her a whack.

THE LILY'S REVENGE

Taylor Mac

An anthropomorphized lily flower longs to be the central character in a play and, to prove it has the talent and drive, imagines an exuberant career.

LILY. Backstage crew cheering. Supporting characters cheering. Old man Joe, who's been pulling the curtain for 80 years, since he was a little boy growing up in the depression working this theater so he could bring home a little money for his mother and sisters to eat. Just a little. Enough to buy a piece of bread and on Christmas a potato. Ever since father died from the tuberculosis. Old Man Joe who has seen over thirty thousand performances in this theater, hardened and callused-hand Old Man Joe is weeping. "Oh Lily, it was the greatest performance this theater has ever seen," "Oh Joe, you don't know what that means to me." Applause. Applause. Applause. Walk backwards. Thanking everyone. Find the railing. Descend the stairs. Open the dressing room door. Thank you. Thank you. Thank you. Applause. Applause. Applause. Gently close door. Muffled sounds of excitement behind the door. Sanctuary. A moment to one's self. Exhale. Put down the flowers. Rest your limbs. Sit in front of the makeup mirror. Look at yourself. Melancholy. A deep sorrow. Alone. Did it happen and if so what does it all mean? And who cares if you're always alone. A knock at the door. Your agent. "Oh darling, you were magnificent." Feign humility. Don't be greedy. Ask her about herself. A knock at the door. The producers. "You were magnificent. Lily, I'd like you to meet insert famous person." "You were magnificent." "Thank you. Thank you. I loved your last picture." "Oh it was nothing to what you do. A real star". "Thank you. Thank you." "Darling, your fans. They await you. Do not keep them waiting in the cold." "Yes you're right." Fur coat. Only a slip on underneath. Pen in hand. To the stage door. Flash. Flash. Screams. Someone faints. Sign. Sign. Sign. Underline the signature. Period. Exclamation point. "We love you. We love you. We love you."

MILKMILKLEMONADE

Joshua Conkel

Cancer-stricken Nanna explains the meaning of life to 11-year-old Emory as she throws chickens into a processing machine.

NANNA. This is why I'm so tough on you. Life is hard, Emory. If you're too soft it just chews you up and spits you out again. That's what separates these chickens from us. See? *(She throws a chicken in.)* Bawk bawk bawk! *(And another.)* They're too stupid to do anything and that's why I get to eat 'em. Now quit buggin' me and let me work!

> *(She throws another chicken in. [*EMORY *rushes to her and grabs her. She pushes him down and throws another chicken in.] She continues to throw chickens in during the following speech. The sound and feathers serve as punctuation.)*

I know I should use this opportunity to teach you a thing or two. Now that I'm in my last days and all. I know I should impart some kind of wisdom about the nature of life and death. I could use metaphors, farming metaphors, about harvests and the changing of seasons, and burning the crops to prepare for a rebirth. But I don't feel like it. *(Throws a chicken in:)* I'm too sick. Emory, there might come a time when you feel so bad it's in every part of you. It's crawling inside of you like ants marching up a tree. That's how I feel today. Like ants are in my veins taking every good feeling I have and toting them off to some hidden place I can't see. This is what I wish somebody would have told me: that some days it hurts so bad to be alive you just wish it would end. People always say that one day you wake up old, wondering where all the years went. But I felt myself getting older. In increments large and small, I felt my body getting rickety. Stiff. My brain getting tired and confused. I wish it had happened in one moment. But it didn't. It took my whole life and it hurt like hell. Now bring me that chicken.

THE MISANTHROPE

adapted by Timothy Mooney

FROM THE PLAY BY MOLIÈRE

Arsinoe (ar-SIN-oh-WAY) drops in on her supposed best friend, the very popular Celimene (SELL-uh-MEN), under the pretense of offering good advice, but cannot resist expressing her own distaste for Celimene's behavior under the guise of citing the harsh opinions of mutual friends. Some suggest that the uptight Arsinoe has a secondary motive: intimidating Celimene to let loose of some of her male companions, including Arsione's crush, the Misanthrope, Alceste.

ARSINOE.

Oh, no, I must be gone.
Madame, the best friend's one who gives support
In matters of the weightiest import.
And we both know there's no subordination
To matters which might touch our reputation.
As such, I've hurried here upon a mission
To tell of talk which threatens your position.
I had a talk last night with just a few
Upstanding folk when topic turned to you.
And though, you know, I instantly defended,
I fear your actions were not well commended.
The looseness of your ways and the parade
Of men who visit you weren't well portrayed.
Your coquetry, I fear's, notorious,
And they spoke in a tone censorious!
I was astounded at this sharp attack,
And in your fair defense I did not lack.
I spoke of your good spirit and I mentioned,
You only have the finest of intentions.
And yet some things I couldn't quite gainsay,
With issues that I can't explain away.
And ultimately, I made the confession
That your behavior gives the wrong impression.
And that your actions may well be the source
Of gossip and conjecture rather coarse.

And that you wouldn't be so oft mistook
If you took greater care for how things look.
It's not that I'm suggesting you're to blame
For deeds the like of which we mustn't name!
But people's minds do tend that way to go,
And we must guard 'gainst vice's slightest show.
I know you know my purity of purpose,
Intending only to do you great service,
I share these thoughts to help my dearest friend,
And have in mind no other hoped-for end.

MISS BETH

Don Zolidis

Coach Tessa delivers an aggressive motivational speech to her cheerleading squad as they prepare themselves for the upcoming Regional Championships.

COACH TESSA. Hold on. I'm about to say something profound. I was on the phone with my husband *[wife]* today. You know what he told me? He said cheering wasn't a sport.

(Shock and horror from the assembled cheerers.)

You know what I said? First, let me say that an attitude like that is why I no longer allow him to be within a fifty-mile radius of me. He circles on the outskirts of town like a rocky asteroid caught in the earth's gravitational pull. But then I said: You know what? You're darn right it's not a sport. It's Life. And.

(She waits for it.)

Death. You think a mere athlete could execute a synchronous twenty-foot seven-twenty twist while looking pert and fresh in makeup? You think a mere athlete could holler in unison and keep pace to the rhythmic, sensuous beats of LMFAO? No. They would tremble and collapse into a spineless puddle of jelly. That's what an athlete would do. You are not women. You are not men. You are Nietzschean super-beings from the future. And I, for one, REJOICE IN YOUR SUPERIORITY! WE WILL NOT YIELD! WE WILL NOT FALTER! WE SHALL RULE!!!!

(Short pause.)

The Regional Conference District Two Cheer Championships in two weeks. That is all.

THE MUSEUM PLAY

Jordan Harrison

Lucy, a guard and a Board Member of the Museum, tells one of the Museum curators the unusual story of how she arrived in her current circumstances.

LUCY. First off Mother dropped me hard on the noggin' right out the starting gates then let me rot my teeth with too much sugar, rot my brain on the teletubby and stay out in the rain too long every night each and every without putting on my rubbers just to teach me a lesson never drink my milk while protecting me from all four basic food groups. Nothing in the house but a trough of candy corn. "One food group," she'd say, pointing. "Eat." Wash the candy down with coca cola (never diet) and I was never to drive careful, she said, or take afternoon naps or play fair or share and by age two I was a pretty spectacular mess.

"Ruined her," Mother said. "Spoiled her with too much love" and she left me here, *abandoned* me over in the Egyptian Wing, abandoned me in an authentic bulrush basket exhibit, Moses-like. Sense of humor on that woman. Funny like a Gila monster. And when Mr. Everly the old Curator found me— "This baby isn't wax like the others!"—he taught me the difference between right and wrong, Phylum and Genus, Jurassic and Paleozoic. Nursed me back to health in the great whirling cornucopia of the cafeteria, made me a featherbed of the stuff they stuff birds with and when I was legal age he put a walkie-talkie in my hand and set me to work, earn my keep, and eventually I worked my way up to a spot on the Board of Directors on account of nobody else attends the meetings and—

I'm sorry, what was the question?

(Astonished silence.)

[**JAME.** You were *raised* in the Museum?]

LUCY. You shouldn't be angry with Mother. I wasn't. She visited every so often, on pay-what-you-wish nights. And on Christmas I'd round up my favorite playmates, the weasel and the dead-as-a dodo and the wildebeestie[1] and we'd gather round the big evergreen in the lobby and oh what a celebration. Carols. I always got to be lead singer, to take the melody, and those were good years. Until the old Curator ran out of breath one day very sudden, almost as if he was singing at notes inaudible to the human ear. *(She makes soundless mouth movements.)* Sort of mysterious. And when *she* came along to replace him, the whole world turned oopsie-daisy.

1 To be pronounced "*Will*-duh-beastie"

NICKY GOES GOTH

Elizabeth Meriwether

Nicky is at a critical crossroads in her adolescence: she's fallen in love with a goth kid from the suburbs. Her older sister, Paris, imparts advice about men, sex, and the "royal" life, in an attempt to set Nicky back on track to the lifestyle of the rich and overexposed.

PARIS. You're going to look beautiful tonight, because here's why. Here's why Nicky. Here's why.

(Tiny moment.)

HERE'S WHY NICKY! I want you to go out there tonight, cut the bullshit, and bring home a boyfriend. Because men are amazing, Nicky, amazing! And they're going to marry us and talk to us, because they're always fucking talking! They talk about, you know, ancient philosophers, they talk about graphs and they make up words and they define words and they pretend to be Christopher Walken and what about all that poison-gas-on-the-subway shit? They're the ones talking about it, Nicky. And I wish I could express my joy…my utter fucking joy… I have all these thoughts, you know, we all do—we're all like wondering all this shit. But it's like as sure as I know that there will be a moon out there and stars and—you know, a fucking sun will come up in the morning or go down at night or come up at night or go down again and then like come back again— I know that there is somewhere this man out there waiting with all the answers to my questions. And he does everything better than me—isn't that fucking amazing, Nicky? There are so many things that men have figured out, Nicky! And they're going to figure out more stuff, and more stuff because they're so right! I can just hear it, all this fucking confidence coming for me…straight for me… Oh god—

(A moment.)

I want to learn how to do metallurgy. I've been thinking about it.

(A moment.)

I love you, Nicky—you're so hot and I love you…

ORANGE LEMON EGG CANARY

Rinne Groff

Henrietta, an old-timey magician's assistant, reveals how she got into the business.

HENRIETTA. It's easy to get stuck. I got stuck the same way it happens to any other person: by accident. I was studying to be a nurse… hey, I could have been a nurse. One day after classes, my friend, my fiancé, if you're a stickler for details, took me to see a Magic Show. Boy oh boy, this magician. He did the usual tricks, the usual stuff—billiard balls, cards, ummmnn, cigarettes, the classics—but it was my first time. I had never seen, I, I, I, had never even heard of a profession like that. I was knocked, completely. I was sitting like this…

(She makes a slight open-mouthed expression.)

That's probably why he chose me, called me to the stage. The stage! Plus he liked to call on girls in the audience who had their boyfriends in tow. Their fiancés. Stickler. He said pick a card, any card. *(Whispering:)* The Queen of Hearts. I held it close to my breast. *(Full-voice again:)* He told me to sit on it. Excuse me? He provided the chair. "Wait," he said, "Face up," and he reached his hand under my thigh. He pulled the card, without looking at it, naturally, flipped it, and slid it back under. Then he asked me to part my lips. Okey-dokey. "Open your mouth wider." Yeah, sure. My fiancé's watching this. He took a small telescope and slipped it inside my open mouth, just a bit, just enough to give me the taste of metal. When I laughed, my teeth came down on it. "Careful," he said. "Be careful." I looked into his eyes. He gazed down my throat, saw straight through every part of my insides, and he guessed my card. He knew my card all right.

And that's what I mean by "stuck."

REVIVAL AT POSSUM KINGDOM COMMUNITY CHURCH

Linda LaRocque

Innocent Ella Faye doesn't meet many people at the Texas bus depot she cleans. However, when two down-on-their-luck con men come along, she eagerly grabs the opportunity to fill their listening ears...with just about anything that comes to mind.

ELLA FAYE. Land of Goshen, it is a hot one today. I swear, this has been the hottest summer I can ever remember. Old Bob Foster's barn caught afire last week. They said it was cause it's so hot. Combustible something or other, I guess. It's just too blame hot to do much work. I work a little and rest a lot in this heat. How about you? You gentlemen warm too? We got sodic pops in the pop cooler by the ticket booth. You can go out and get one if you like. [...]

You sure you gentlemen don't want a sodie? They used to carry only Coke Cola, but just before Decoration Day—or was it just after? Land, I can't remember like I used to, so you'll have to excuse me. But anyway, it was around Decoration Day we'll say, and the big old Nee Hi Orange sodie pop truck was coming down the highway out here and Fern Preston's bull was loose, and ran right in the middle of the road. Now we all know Fern's bull is a mean devil, but he was no match for that Nee Hi truck. But he stood right there in the middle of the road and never moved. Scared the fire out of the poor truck driver. He hit the brakes and that big old truck started a lurching and a swaying and it tipped clean over. And Nee Hi Orange sodie was a flying everywhere and Fern Preston's bull went a running for home with his tail between his legs for sure. I heard the screeching. Was sitting right here in fact. We all went a running to see what happened. Me, Otto—that's the ticket taker—and the Russell twins—they was here getting a Coke Cola. There was pop, bottles, and broken glass from here to kingdom come. So we picked up what wasn't broke, brought it back here, stuck it in the cooler. Oh, the driver said we could. And we sold em all in two weeks. Folks like it better than Coke Cola. Some folks, that is, like it better. So from then on we started carrying Nee Hi. Now, would you care for one?

STRETCH (A FANTASIA)

Susan Bernfield

Ohio, 2004. Rose Mary Woods, President Nixon's longtime secretary (who famously testified to mistakenly erasing part of an 18 ½-minute gap in the Watergate tapes) is nearing the end of her life. In this fantasy sequence, a vigorous Rose dreams she was a very different kind of secretary.

ROSE. I dream I am the secretary.
Of State.

(Typewriter sounds go out.)

Which is strange 'cause we never set much store
by that particular office, but this is a dream and so I—

(Sound cue: classical piano music.)

Not that Condi Rice—
who I hear's next if…
That gal always looks so worried
and she only tells the boss
what he wants to hear.

No! I'm that other one, the other one
that Madame—Madeleine Albright!

(Sound cue: music changes to a brass band, perhaps, with processional or state dinner-ish music.)

That's a sturdy woman, that's someone
of substance
someone who's lived a life.
That's a woman to make a woman proud
that a woman is Secretary of State.
She looks damn organized, too.
Or—*I* do.

I, Madame Secretary, travel the world
in as dignified a manner as possible

I am a crack negotiator. I can be…diplomatic.
Or not:

I don't like your tie.

(She laughs, loud.)

In the gilt-edged, red velvet chairs
of the world
I sit 4.5 precise feet from my rainbow of counterparts
the flashbulbs pop and I smile a serious smile
that says—*we haven't finished talking.*
I sit up straight, feel my substance, my sub-stan-tiality
from the top of my prodigious head stuffed with facts
to the golden throat where my multi-layered voice resides—
indeed, I speak in chords!
From my bosom concealed under a tasteful red suit
to my thick calves and practical pumps.

I squeeze all that substance into pantyhose every damn day
of my life.
That's the kind of thing people just don't get credit for!
Whether they're a secretary or Secretary of State!
Whether they're any of the sweeties who gather round our current guy
that Condi and Harriet and Karen Hughes—
they're just so *smitten* those girls, have ya noticed that?
A man is lucky to have those girls
those girls'll do anything, anything for—
but I digress.
I'm Madame Secretary
Secretary of Madeleine State!
Packing my bag and traveling the world
packing a punch
packing the diplomatic core
of my being
which extrudes from my pantyhosed fancy exterior
I am—
I have—
I speak for the President. I do, I really do.

THE TWELVE DATES OF CHRISTMAS

Ginna Hoben

Newly single and recovering from a broken engagement, Mary engages in a one-night stand with a younger man. Somewhat embarrassed, she then attempts to justify her actions to the audience.

MARY. My new friend Maggie loves St. Patrick's Day. Probably because it is the only occasion on which she feels justified to drink her weight in beer. And whiskey. Like thousands of other Americans do on this day, we both shamelessly multiply our Irish heritage beyond its truthful percentage and trounce from one Irish pub to another. It is convenient that we both live on the Upper West Side, just two blocks from "Alcohol Alley"—Amsterdam between 75th and 85th. We start at McAleer's, move to George Keely's, and then to The Dead Poet where we happily screech to a halt under the caring hands of the young and adorable, authentically Irish bartender, Aidan O'Reilly.

(Beat.)

Young Aidan has been in the States for under a year, which evidently is not long enough to become disenchanted with drunken American females. Between pouring us shots of Jameson, we talk about books and films and plays; he's so clever, I feel wittier by association. At the end of the night Maggie's new boyfriend Jay comes to scrape us off our bar stools, but I can't stop thinking about the hot ass on the bartender ten years too young for me. The bar closes and Young Aidan meets me on the sidewalk out front. As Maggie and Jay drive off in their cab, I hear her scream "don't forget Personal Policy Number Five!"

(Beat.)

Okay. So. P.P. Number Five. For many years I have upheld the personal policy: "Do not sleep with anyone whose ass is smaller than yours." But. Shut. Up. A butt as perfect as this one is born to break policies. I have also, for many years, upheld the policy that I will not sleep with anyone who is more than ten years older or younger than me.

(Beat.)

Ladies and Gentlemen. There is no good reason why a woman in her thirties should deny herself the pleasure of sleeping with a man in his twenties.

(Beat.)

All right, I know I should feel a little ashamed.

(Sheepish.)

I am way too old for one-night stands. With a bartender.

(Cringe.)

On St. Patrick's Day.

(Pulling herself together.)

For the record, I do not delude myself that episodes like this will gain me the love I want and deserve. It's really quite the opposite; that by giving my time and energy to meaningless…*relationships*…I am actually sacrificing the time and space where a healthy, mature partnership could thrive.

(Sigh.)

I am not proud of my actions.

(Beat.)

I feel embarrassed to have admitted any of this out loud.

(Beat.)

And if I could go back in time…I would do it all again!

THE WOMAN WHO AMUSES HERSELF

Victor Lodato

Miss Mattel, a third-grade schoolteacher, gives her class a lesson on Leonardo da Vinci's Mona Lisa. *In doing so, she inevitably reveals something of her own frustrations and longings.*

MISS MATTEL. Can you see back there? *(She turns to look at the screen.)* Oh. Jimmy, Jimmy—you have the slide in upside down. *(Looks out into the audience.)* Take it out, put it in the other way. *(She turns to look back at the screen, which goes blank for a moment, then is filled with the projection, correctly positioned but still out of focus.)* Alright, now focus it—she looks like she's been through the wash. *(The image grows even more blurry.)* Jimmy. You're killing her. The other way. Turn the dial the other way. *(She looks back into the audience, annoyed.)* Watch what you're doing, Jimmy. Watch the screen while you turn the dial, so that you can *see* what your *hand* is doing. *(She looks back at the screen; the image slowly comes into focus.)* Right there, stop. Perfect. Let go of the dial. *(Back out to audience:)* Thank you, Jim. Now, go sit down—take your seat. *(Pause.)* Alright, everybody. This painting... Yes, Kate I'm sure you have seen it... *(A bit strained:)* Oh, how nice—last summer, really? ...No, I've never been to France, never been. *(Pause.)* Okay, everybody: this painting is a very famous work of art. Painted at the beginning of the sixteenth century by Leonardo da Vinci. Does anyone know what it's called? Not you, Kate... Yes, Mark... That's right: The *Mona Lisa* ... No, she doesn't have two names; *Mona* is short in Italian for *Madonna,* my lady—so the title is something like calling her Lady Lisa—or Mrs. Lisa. Because she was a married woman—or so it is believed. Young wife to a rich man. Not a bad deal. Lisa de Giocondo. In Italy, they call the painting *La Gioconda*—which is very interesting because this means two things: It means that she is the wife of this Giocondo, but it also means, if one translates it, "the woman who amuses herself." ...What is so funny, Mr. Hoster? Mr. Funnypants? *(She regards a student sternly, points a finger at him.)* None of that. I am warning you. *(Pause.)* Alright, now: This painting is so famous because, before this, no one had really ever given such incredible expression to the human face in art. With this portrait, you really can feel—look at it, kids—you really can feel that there are things going on in this woman's head. You can feel that there is a big life beyond this little moment. I know I do. This woman has hopes and dreams and secrets. You get a sense—don't you?—that this woman is not going to just let her life pass her by, mindlessly, in a rich man's house—but that she is going to embrace life to the fullest, even if sometimes it's a little sad. Because, I think there's a little sadness there, too. A little bit. Can't you picture her, at night, a hundred thoughts in her head, she can't sleep, she gets up, all by herself, takes a walk in the garden? I know I've done it. *(Pause.)* Look at the expression on her face. Those confident eyes. That little *perky* smile. They say that Leonardo worked on this painting for many, many years—and that when he had Mrs. Lisa sit for him, there would be musicians playing beautiful music—flutes and lyres—so that she would be able to maintain that wonderful expression. And sometimes someone would read a little poetry. Sing a little song… Well, I don't know what the songs were back then. Something festive. The point is the music played, and she held that expression—and Leonardo recorded it. One of those *rare* instances of a man really understanding a woman. Because, I'm telling you, *that* does not happen very often. *(Pause.)* Now, I want you to look at what she's wearing: dark colors, a black veil. What a person wears when someone has died. And in the little that is known about this woman, we know that one of her children—a boy—died when he was very young. We come back to the sadness. Maybe this painting was begun while she was still in mourning—and maybe the musicians were an attempt to distract her from her grief. We don't really know. And that's kind of wonderful, though—to *not* know. To make up one's own story. *(Pause.)* And that is what I want each of you to do.

DRAMA

25 QUESTIONS FOR A JEWISH MOTHER

Kate Moira Ryan and Judy Gold

A Chinese-American social worker who converted to Judaism for her husband responds to a question about her biggest regret.

WOMAN #5. My biggest regret? People have asked me do I regret converting? Well, there are a lot of parallels between being Jewish and being Chinese. In Chinese culture sons are revered and girls are second class citizens. And the number one rule they share is—don't embarrass me in public. I am from both cultures. Honest. I am a Modern Orthodox Chinese Jewish woman. I am the second daughter of Chinese immigrants. I am a rebel. I met my husband in a bookstore in San Francisco and after a couple of dates he said, "I would like to marry someone Jewish." So I found an Orthodox rabbi in Berkeley and studied with him for two years and then we got married. Afterwards, I would run into my mother's friends who would say, "Theresa, I have boy for you." She had told no one I had gotten married. I remained an embarrassment to my mother until her death. Even though I was the only one of her six children to graduate from college. After my marriage I worked as a social worker in San Francisco. I did a lot of home care visits to the elderly. I knocked on one door. A woman opened it and she said to me, "Mrs. Weinstein?" and I said to her, "Mrs. Wong?" You see she was white and I'm Chinese. It's not often you find someone living your parallel life. I loved San Francisco, I hated leaving it. My husband wanted us to come to New Jersey. He wanted the kids to go to Jewish school here and he said that we wouldn't stand out so much. But, the truth is I never felt like a minority until I came here. One man shouted at me, "Hey chink!" I said to him, "Are you talking to me?" He said, "Yeah, don't you know who you are?" But that's not who I am. I don't ever regret converting to Judaism, but I regret moving here. I hate New Jersey. I don't belong here.

25 QUESTIONS FOR A JEWISH MOTHER

Kate Moira Ryan and Judy Gold

A special education teacher and mother of two has just been asked about her favorite woman in the Bible.

WOMAN #7. Miriam. In the Bible God chose her along with her brother Moses to lead the Israelites out of Egypt. She was considered a prophetess. I liked her strong and forceful nature and she was resourceful. I found her almost a feminist hero, if a feminist hero can be found in the Bible. When I first got pregnant with Micah, I told my mother and she refused to let me visit her when I started to show. She lived in this middle class housing project in Brooklyn and she didn't want her neighbors to see me pregnant. I think in her eyes what I was doing was disgraceful and shameful. Then we had Micah and she went gaga. Right after he was born, I brought him over to mother's apartment. I got on the elevator with a neighbor who had known me since I was a little girl. She looked at Micah and then looked at me and said, "I didn't know you got married." And when I told her I didn't, she began to shout at me, "If you were my daughter, I would have thrown you out." And this went on for twenty-one floors. When I finally got to my mother's apartment, I handed Micah to my mother and I told her about the neighbor and what she said. And my mother said, "She's ignorant. She's sick in the head." I took Micah back from her and I nearly shouted, "What about you? What about you not wanting me to visit when I was pregnant?" And my mother's eyes filled with tears. She didn't say anything, but I knew at last that I had made my point. I like Miriam because she led her people through the desert and sometimes, in a small way when I look at my children, I feel as though I am doing the same thing, except my desert is ignorance and intolerance.

110 STORIES

Sarah Tuft

Ordinarily an actor and waitress at a fine restaurant—now a 9/11 volunteer—Michelle discovers how it feels to "be of service" while giving out water at Ground Zero.

MICHELLE WYLDE WILLIAMS. I woke up not sure how I was going to spend my day until I found myself washing yesterday's asbestos out of my hair so I wouldn't get a double layer of it. [...] Then I head to the Salvation Army again, where the loading of way too many supplies is spilling onto the sidewalks. Finally a Major tells me to wait off to the side. They can't tell anyone a van's headed down to Ground Zero because the volunteers would literally riot at the idea of some going and others staying. Craziness. Soon, we all have badges and are headed down. The next few hours are just like last night, offering water and Gatorade to man after man—and the very occasional woman—and all of them waving me away or accepting and always saying, not just, "Thank you," but "Thank you very much." One guy said, "No thank you. But you are a vision!" And at that moment, I so wanted to be the most beautiful woman in the world, the loveliest person alive—a distraction on any level. Maybe, just maybe, for that one moment, I was. I've never been surrounded by more men in my life. I've never been the only woman as far as the eye could see, with every man in uniform no less. I've never been a woman who thinks a man in uniform is appealing. Of course, none of this is appealing. But these men are all so respectful, so grateful. Many of them met and held my eyes longer than they normally would have, not searching really but definitely, definitely connecting. But everyone holds hugs longer these days. Everyone touches more.

ACTS OF GOD

Mark Rigney

High-school student Kim recalls the night an F-3 tornado destroyed Prairie Sunset, her trailer park neighborhood.

KIM. I wasn't home the night of the tornado. I had a half-shift at *[insert name of local grocery store]* and I was just getting off. I got in my car. My cell rang. I wish I hadn't answered. The I.D. said it was Wayne. Wayne, who doesn't look anything like Kenny Chesney, and I didn't want to talk. I figured he was wantin' me to come over, even though it was a school night—for me. Not for him. Wayne's oldest kid is twelve! So obviously it was time to break it off. And I was tired and angry and I didn't want to be pushed into the breakup speech, 'cos I've had that done, and it sucks, but I answered, I figured, "I'll just get it over with." God! Why did I pick up? See, Wayne had a ranch house, like a half-mile from Prairie Sunset. His thing was restoring old Mustangs, mostly at night, 'cos he's like a serious insomniac. He'd heard a storm was coming, and the sump pump was busted, so he figured—like me with the breakup—might as well get it over with. So down he went…

[…]

…but when the storm hit, the house kind of jumped off its foundation, and he got wedged underneath, legs squashed, arms pinned. He could just reach his cell phone. I knew right off something was wrong, 'cos he said, "Hi, Kim. D'you mind if I maybe call you Kim tonight?" Which he never does. To him, I'm always Kimmie. I said, "Wayne, what's wrong?" And he said, "Well, just one little thing, really. But it'll prob'ly be enough." The thing is, see, he was testing the pump, filling up the sump pit with a hose, and the hose was still on, it's still pumping in water, so the water's rising, and his head—he's got his head hanging in over the lip of the pit, and he can't move. He's got a joist or something pressing down on his neck. So I'm talking to him, right, in my very dry, very safe car in the *[insert local grocery store name]* parking lot, and he's watching the water rising up right toward his face, rising like an inch a minute, and I go, "Did you dial 9-1-1?" and he says, "I did, and they're swamped." So I'm on the other line, right? 9-1-1!

I'm *screaming* for police. I give them the exact location, but it's chaos, there're people in trouble all over the place, roads blocked, trees down, and I switch back to Wayne and I can hear the water over the phone line. I can *still* hear it…it sounds like a dishwasher. And then Wayne, he says, "Kim, it's okay. It's okay, you did everything you could. This isn't your fault, all right? Not your fault. And maybe this is good, 'cos you can't hang around with me. I'd wreck your life." And I try to interrupt, but he says, "No, I'm gonna hang up the phone. You don't have to say 'Good-bye' or anything you don't want to. Just, you know, tell my kids I love 'em, yeah? Because, you know what? Everything really is going to be okay." But it's *not* okay! How can what happened to Wayne be okay? "Okay" means normal, "Okay" means it happens every day—and I don't give a flying crap that he would have wrecked my life! He was so wrong. Everything okay? No. I am terrified of telephones and nothing is okay.

AJAX IN IRAQ

Ellen McLaughlin

Debbie is an American soldier stationed in Iraq during the Iraq War. She speaks about the confusion surrounding the U.S. mission, expressing the profound frustration so many soldiers feel at the lack of articulation as to why the troops are being asked to put their lives at risk.

DEBBIE. So we're out here getting our asses shot off and so forth, all this terror going down. Years now this has been going on, years. So why are we here? Why are we fighting this thing? You tell me. No really. It's not like I haven't asked. I've asked. I ask everyone I meet. Maybe 200 soldiers at this point—every level of the military. You know what? Nobody fucking knows. Or really what it is is everybody knows but they know completely different things. You ask every single person in a unit and each one has a different answer. We're here to give them democracy, to give them capitalism, to help them keep their oil, to take their oil, to help them fight each other, to keep them from fighting each other, to get them all to fight somebody else, to control the Sunni, to destroy the Sunni, to control the Shia, to destroy the Shia, because we're in the pocket of the Saudis, because we don't want to be in the pocket of the Saudis, because Bush wanted to do his Daddy's war again and get it right this time, because Bush was so stupid he picked the wrong country to attack after 9/11 and now we have to stay here, um, protecting "American interests" in Iraq... Which means what? We're, like, driving these refrigerated trucks full of army meals and energy drinks around at 80 miles an hour, risking IEDs and worse, and we're basically here to what? Protect the energy drinks? But you know, that's what it feels like sometimes. 'Cause the energy drinks are real, just like the bombs and the mortars are real, and, well, Freedom? Democracy?—not so much. All I'm saying is, we don't have a fucking clue what we're laying our lives down for here. So I keep asking. Because I'd really like to know.

BY THE WATERS OF BABYLON

Robert Schenkkan

Austin, Texas. A chance encounter brought Catherine and Arturo together—two exiles from two very different worlds, both haunted. A day of drinking and dancing and intimacy now brings Catherine face to face with her ghosts.

CATHERINE. Yes. He would still hurt me. But I could make him feel ashamed. Just by looking at him. For once, I had a kind of power over him and I would use it—God, would I use it! One night, after what he thought of as sex, he got up out of bed and fell. Right there.

(Points to spot on the floor.)

Heart attack. I was wide awake. Just the way he liked me. I got up to call the hospital and then—I stopped. He saw what I was thinking. *I know,* he saw what I was thinking. He tried to say something but—He was in a lot of pain. *I hope.* Face twisted. Swollen. This terrible, raw, throaty sound ripping out of him. I sat down, in that chair, and I watched him die. At the end, this strange—this *terrible* thing—happened. He smiled at me. And there was something—satisfied—in that smile. I had this—awful feeling that I was now—*his*—in a way I had never been before. *And forever.* I made sure he was dead. Then…

*(*CATHERINE *gestures vaguely.)*

[…]

They were amazingly fast. *(Scathing:)* Why not, this isn't East Austin; important people live here; decent people! One of the paramedics, this young man, asked me what happened. He had a nose ring with a little blue bead on it. I had this wild urge to touch it; ask him if it hurt. I couldn't tell him the truth, of course. I was asleep, I said. I woke up; heard a noise. Found my husband on the floor. Called right away. I could tell he didn't believe me. The neighbors were all watching as they rolled Edgar out. Mrs. Stilson. Nancy. George. I tried to look appropriately—distressed—but *I wanted to laugh.* Only I knew if I started, I wouldn't be able to stop. There was an autopsy. Questions were raised. I was never actually charged but—word got out.

THE CHERRY ORCHARD

translated by Nicholas Saunders and Frank Dwyer

FROM THE PLAY BY ANTON CHEKHOV

Lyubov Andreyevna is the owner of a large Russian country estate with a famous cherry orchard. She has been living out of the country for the last five years, but she has been called home by her brother and daughters to deal with a crisis. Unless they can come up with the money to pay the mortgage, their beloved ancestral home will be sold at auction.

Lopakhin, a wealthy young entrepreneur whose father and grandfather were serfs on the estate, is grateful to Lyubov Andreyevna for the kindness she showed him when he was a boy. He has a plan to help her: she must give up the estate, allow the old house and orchard to be knocked down, and build cottages for summer rentals on the site. That income would save them, but Lopakhin cannot get her and her brother Gayev to think about the problem, much less discuss a practical solution. They're so afraid of the future they can only talk about the past, or try to distract themselves in the present.

LYUBOV ANDREYEVNA. We are paying for our sins… […] So many sins…I wasted all my money, threw it away like a woman possessed. I married a man who brought me nothing but debts. He killed himself with champagne—drank himself to death—and then, to my everlasting sorrow, I fell in love again, and I held nothing back, I gave myself again, and just as I did—my first punishment came, it fell like a thunderbolt—my little boy drowned…right here, in the river. So I ran away, far away, for good I thought—I never meant to come back, never wanted to see this river again…I was mad with grief, I closed my eyes, I tried to shut everything out—but he came after me…thinking only of himself, of course, without pity or mercy…I bought a villa near Menton, for his sake, because he fell ill there, and for three years I nursed him, night and day. I had no rest. He wore me out, body and soul—he sucked the life out of me. Last year the villa was sold for debts. We moved to Paris, and that's where he robbed me, cast me aside and left me for another. I tried to poison myself…oh, how stupid, shameful…and then suddenly I felt a longing to see my country again, my Russia, and my little girl… *(She wipes away her tears.)* Forgive me, dear

Father in Heaven! Have mercy on me! Don't punish me any more! *(She takes a telegram from her pocket.)* This came today, from Paris. He's sorry, he wants me to come back… *(She tears up the telegram.)* Is that music? *(She listens.)*

THE DIARY OF A TEENAGE GIRL

Marielle Heller

ADAPTED FROM THE GRAPHIC NOVEL BY PHOEBE GLOECKNER

It's the 1970s in San Francisco and Minnie, 15, is trying to cope with her environment: she is having an affair with her mother's boyfriend, living under the guardianship of her drug-abusive mother, and dealing with the sexual feelings and frustrations of growing up. As an outlet, Minnie records her diary on an old tape player when she is alone.

MINNIE. Dear Diary, I did not go to school today. I was expelled again. I walked down to Polk Street.

(She walks. Slowly.)

I feel very sad and lonely, and the only one who can offer surcease from my sorrow is that beautiful young lesbian outside of Bob's Grill.

(The shadow of a girl crosses the stage mysteriously. Something odd happens. MINNIE *shivers.)*

She is so beautiful, and smiles so sweetly, I could cry.

*(*MINNIE *looks at the girl and realizes she's looking back.* MINNIE *looks around, and waves shyly.)*

Oh my heart. Could I ever love a girl?

I feel so awkward and ugly and naïve and lonely. Maybe I should kill myself maybe I should paint a picture. I should paint a picture. I always want to be touched. I don't know what's wrong with me.

*(*MINNIE *goes back to her room and flops on the bed.)*

I am seriously considering running away. I mean it. My mother is constantly miserable and she's always entertaining her low-life friends. Stone-y Burt. Michael Cocaine. Mom and Andrea got some coke from Michael Cocaine and it gave them the energy to clean the house all day today. Now they're making dinner.
(Singing:) I gotta get out of this place! If it's the last thing I ever do...

DOG ACT

Liz Duffy Adams

A post-apocalyptic future. Vera Similitude, a traveling vaudevillian, reveals to her young companion Jo Jo her plot to kill Zetta, another wandering entertainer, during an upcoming performance.

VERA. *(Rapidly:)* I would have thought even your small wit could have puzzled that out without a pause for exposition. But, attend, I will illumine: we have lost our cart and everything we need to live; Zetta will share, up to a point, but it is her cart and her properties and her sufferance; they could chase us off whenever they pleased, and we would revert instantly to desperate need; not to mention that I am no one's supporting player. It is true that I could take it all, but slowly, so she would not know at what moment it ceases to be hers and becomes mine; I could enslave her, as I have her mongrel, without spilling a salty droplet. I have done it before. But I am no longer as patient as I once was, I am not patient at all and I will have it, I will take it, I will not wait. Marauders are at the gate again and we must be ready. So. Yes? Do you understand? May we go on now? When we come to The Tower scene, when you come on as the plagues, switch the prop knife: let your blade be real, and let it be swift. The dog won't hinder you. Then when your Scavengers show up they can have her body to recycle. Instead of yours. Go on, now. Prepare.

FLOAT

Patricia Kane

Doodee has accidentally intercepted a flirtatious phone call from her husband, Hoot, to her fellow Women's Club member Char, a middle-aged, Midwestern real estate agent. Char attempts to explain the situation.

CHAR. Doodee… […] Doodee. There's nothing going on. Nothing besides a man in middle-age crisis doing his best to rekindle some kind of—I don't know—"virility" by flirting with "the divorcee" in town who desperately needs a sale. He called me two weeks ago and said he was interested in that land I've got listed off Route 23, and I admit, I have been willing to sell my soul some along with the property…by letting him talk a little…you know—but it has not gone beyond that and it wouldn't. I promise you. Doodee, Jack left me for another woman. I know what that pain is. It tears a hole inside you that never heals. Should I have put a stop to this silliness immediately? Absolutely. But, Doodee, between you and me, I haven't had a sale in months. I'm just limping along, and my judgment's clouded with desperation, I guess. But that's not an excuse. I know you and I, we aren't close, but please know that I wouldn't hurt you for the world. And I would never do to another woman what was done to me. That is just about the lowest form of human life in my estimation. But, maybe sometimes the thing you most desperately don't want to become is the thing that's laid in your lap. That's not an excuse either. It's just…oh, I am talking way too much. I'm gonna stop now. Please say something.

(A long beat.)

[…] Doodee… […]

(Beat.)

Ok. *(*CHAR *picks up her coat.)* What happened here tonight—as far as I'm concerned—it doesn't leave this barn. I'm sorry, Doodee. I hope you can forgive me. *(*CHAR *starts to exit.)* And I hope you can forgive Hoot. He's not a bad man, Doodee. And he loves you. He does. You're a good team. He's just…thrown right now by what he sees in the mirror. He wants his old self, his old spark back. That's all. That's all.

FULL BLOOM

Suzanne Bradbeer

Phoebe is a sensitive and precocious 15-year-old who has blossomed over the summer into a physical beauty. After a frightening experience in Italy, she tries to cope with the attention her new appearance is causing.

PHOEBE. There was something about that trip to Italy that I didn't mention, I don't know why. Now it's pretty much the only thing I remember.

I took a lot of walks by myself. Whenever I could, wherever we were. Which wasn't as often as I wanted because the Sabatinis are very conscientious people. I got tired of being around them, and very tired of Steffani. Anyway, near the end of the trip I slipped out of the hotel during our afternoon 'quiet-time.' I was walking along the Via Ricasoli—in Florence—when these guys started following me. I didn't notice them at first because I'd been thinking about the David and Michelangelo. I used to want to be an artist. Mom says it's almost like I go into a trance when I think about stuff like that. So these guys were very close to me before I noticed them, and suddenly they sort of…forced me into this side street. Not by touching me, but by just… surrounding me. They were so close I couldn't see past them. I thought I was going to get raped or mutilated for sure, and I felt like such a jerk for letting them corner me like that. There were four or five of them, talking, gesturing, looking me up and down, I couldn't, breathe. And then it dawned on me: it was like they were *admiring* me. I almost felt like I should feel *complimented.*

They never touched me.

They were just admiring me. And that's good, right? That's good.

THE GARDENS OF AZTLAN

Luis Alfaro

La Karmine has left her monotonous, underappreciated job working as a tortilla maker for a chain restaurant in Southern California. She meets other tortilleras and together they search to reclaim their lost heritage.

LA KARMINE. I shouldn't have left.

(She looks back at the El Torito.)

It's not so bad in there.
At least I get an apron.
I couldn't do it anymore.
I love these tortillas too much.
I mean, no one appreciates my tortillas.
Especially at El Torito.
They grab my tortillas like they grab for the chips.
No feeling.
Something so warm and they lunge at it.
They spread the guacamole and the salsa so thick,
you don't even recognize the pobre tortilla.
What they do to a tortilla is just criminal.
Look at my tortillas.
Mira.

(She throws some, like frisbees, at the audience.)

Every single one has my body, my work, my amor attached to it.
I started to resent them.
Those tortilla abusers.
Not even abusers really.
Because they don't even get to know the tortilla.
Tortilla Ignorers.
At first, I used to feel sorry for them.
'They're hungry,' I would think to myself.
'They can't help it.'
But then, you get politicized to the plight of the tortilla.
And you build an anger.

Adentro de ti.
They dismiss us.
Our trabajo.
They don't even see us as a gente some times.
We have a history, que no?
I know that there isn't a Tortilla Hall of Fame, but that doesn't mean that we are not important.
We're necessary.
Try eating frijoles with your hands…
Yes, try.
Look at my hands.
They are flatter now.
The better to shape the circle of my tortillas.
No beginning and no end to the tortilla.
Just a circle.
A constant.
A world with no end.
A tortilla with no end.
I won't hate them, though.
Because that would be like hating my tortillas.
I love my tortillas.
I know that might seem like a cliché these days.
Tortillas hecho a mano.
Have you ever heard that?
It's a very special thing.
It's like a Walt Whitman poem, "Leaves of Tortillas."
There has to be a place para mi out there in el mundo.
A place where I can make my little half dozen and share them with gente que quiere appreciate them.
Where do we go when our corazones get so heavy with the world that we can't see our lugar in it anymore?
How do I find mi amor of the tortillera once again?
How do I find myself en el mundo, otra vez?
El Torito has been good to me.
I mean, they give dinero to teatros and all,
but there has to be a place, un lugar,
in the world where tortillas reign.
So, here I am.
I came to a place.
To something natural.

Something untouched.
Nature.
Me dicen que all of this was orange groves.
Si, rows and rows of oranges falling all over la tierra.
A sea of pulp and rind.
Pero, I can't find it.
This place.
This place of the naranja where we first were found.
'Found.'
As if we needed to be discovered.
We already had tortillas,
what more did we need?
It's here somewhere, que no?
Right under us.
From now on,
me voy a quedar aqui
and make my tortillas.
I am going to make my tortillas in nature.
Until I see a naranja.
Just one…

(She looks out at the jardin.)

GLADYS IN WONDERLAND

Rosemary Frisino Toohey

Doris is grappling with the mental deterioration of her elderly mother. She fantasizes about what it will be like when death finally ends this difficult chapter.

DORIS. I feel guilty about Mom all the time now and it's wearing me down. Ken wanted me to go with him on a business trip to relax, get away. So I got a woman from an agency to come by, and I had my cousin stop in and check, just to be sure everything was okay. Still, the whole time we were gone I had just one thought. What if something happens? I lived through it over and over in my mind. The hotel phone would ring and someone would say… Doris, your mother died. Then we'd fly home and I'd make the arrangements.

(Pause.)

I could see myself standing in the funeral parlor, people coming up to me, taking my hand, so sorry, Doris, we're so sorry. And I'd say thank you, thank you for coming. Over and over I'd say it. But deep inside there'd be this tiny voice saying, it's over. It's finally over. And I'd never have to walk into that house again and see her with her hair all wild and her blouse buttoned backward.

(Pause.)

Even so, I could feel myself breaking into pieces at the thought of it. Messed-up hair, wrinkled duster, and all the rest, my mother would be gone. Gone for good. Gone forever. Gone.

(Pause.)

But nothing happened. We were away four days and when we got back she was still there, waiting for my voice on the phone, my key in the door.

(Pause.)

She raised me to tackle my difficulties, grapple with my problems, but this one…I just don't know. And it is my problem. She doesn't think she has a problem.

GRETTY GOOD TIME

John Belluso

Gretty is a 32-year-old paralyzed polio victim living in a nursing home. She remembers learning of the death of her estranged brother, Puppy.

GRETTY. That evening. In the ugly walls.

The ugly walls large with blue and white tile
The nurse touched my arm and said we must talk
She stared downward and held back a small smile
Death on her mind, her skin was poison chalk

"He's dead" and I felt a shift from inside
My mouth filled with stones, no scream or no shout
My belly was all swelled, my neck, my side
A creature's movement, pushing it's way out

Such pressure from within, horrendous might
The pain began to move up from my hips
Huge my head was, and my skin stretched so tight
Eyes with dark fear and opening my lips

(Softly singing:)

Out spit pieces of coal, slivers of shale
Then mouth stretched further, and out slipped, a whale.

[**HIDEKO.** A whale.]

GRETTY. Yes. Giant sea creature, whale, from my mouth, now on the floor in front of me, pointing its head towards the sun, it was crying, horrible sounds, its body began flailing, breaking the chairs, crushing the floor boards. Stinking. And I thought: This doesn't belong here. It's too big. It's too much. The weight, the weight of this creature's body will crush everything, it will crush everyone I love. Like it crushed my Puppy. It doesn't belong here.

*(*GRETTY *uses her arm to push her body out of the wheelchair, she falls to the ground. [*DR. HENRY *finished preparing the syringe and needle; the injection to end Gretty's life.])*

It doesn't belong here.

(She uses her arm to drag her body through the sand, towards the waves.)

And I thought: I will not carry this beast. I will drag it through the pebbles and sand. I will drag it into the ocean foam, I will bury it deep within the sea, where it belongs.

HELEN

adapted by Ellen McLaughlin

FROM THE PLAY BY EURIPIDES

In this rethinking of the Euripides play, Helen of Troy never went to Troy at all, (she was replaced by a "cloud copy" mischievously made by the gods) but has spent the last seventeen years in a hotel in Egypt, wild with frustration at not knowing any details about the war that she knows has been fought in her name. (She doesn't get much cable on her television and she never leaves her room.) Athena, Goddess of War, terrifying in her regalia, magnificent in her cynicism, visits Helen and tells her that the war (which sounds a lot like the First World War) has been over for seven years and that, despite its spectacular devastation, the gods lost interest in it after a few weeks. She then lets her in on the secret of why the gods created human beings in the first place.

ATHENA. You're too much, kid. *(She chuckles, almost affectionate.)* You know what we love about you people? You die. And that means you've all got stories. That's why we came up with you. Even the dullest mortal life has a beginning, middle and an end. It's so fucking poignant. It could be that the whole Trojan War was just a big fat dramaturgical mistake on our parts. Way too tidy. Our desire to wrap everything up with a single enormous blowout just ended up diluting all the stories down to one unsatisfying truncated shrug of a narrative. I mean, it's not like it's your *fault,* but we lost respect for you guys. You just looked like so many panicked beetles scrambling around on that dung hill. Or maybe it was the monotony of the deaths that got to us. Not that there wasn't a lot of *variety*—we could watch people get blown to bits by bombs, cut down like wheat by machine gun fire slicing across rows of stumbling men; [...] oh, there were *variations...* But really when all was said and done, it was just a whole heck of a lot of death. And it turns out that death makes human *life* interesting. But that death *itself* isn't particularly interesting. Because you all die the same way. Looking surprised. It's amazing. Here you are the only creature on earth who knows you're going to die—it colors your entire existence from your earliest moments of consciousness. You can even spend years on a battlefield, watching *other* people die left and right of you, but when your *own* death comes, *as you always knew it would,* you're still, like, "What? ME? Surely you don't mean ME!" *(Amused:)* It kills us.

HIDDEN: STORIES FROM THE DUTCH RESISTANCE

Jamie Bruss and Christopher Willard

Present-day United States. Miriam, feisty and wise, describes her experience in prison as a member of the Dutch Resistance against Hitler's Nazi regime.

MIRIAM. Now, this is better. It can get cold out on the porch.

(She consults the clock.)

We still have a little while before we have to get ready. Are you comfortable enough? I can't seem to relax at the moment. I don't mind speaking about these things; I just can't do it sitting down.

(Beat.)

If you were in the resistance, you didn't tell anyone what you were doing. Not your husband, not your wife. If, God forbid, they were caught, the less they knew, the less they might be forced to reveal. You had to always be on your guard.

(Beat.)

I got overconfident once. It got me arrested. I was transporting too much food and didn't have the proper documentation. I always thought I inherited my mother's capacity to tolerate anything. Six months in prison showed me otherwise.

(Beat, holding her arm:)

They interrogated me for three days straight, once. They left me alone in a room—with a knife on the table. Did they want me to try and escape so they could shoot me—or use the knife on myself? I weighed my decision for what seemed like an eternity.

(Beat.)

And then I noticed a radio on the table. The Germans had outlawed radios. Too many people were listening to the Allied broadcasts. I hadn't heard music in a very long while.

(She turns on the radio. We hear Verdi's "Chorus of the Hebrew Slaves.")

There was something stirring in that music. Hopeful. It saved my life that day.

HIDDEN: STORIES FROM THE DUTCH RESISTANCE

Jamie Bruss and Christopher Willard

Siena, a nurse in Nazi-occupied Holland, describes her decision to stay and care for the Jewish children being held in a nursery-turned-deportation-center before each child is shipped off to an uncertain place and future.

SIENA. There is a theatre across from the creche. I went there once to see an opera by Verdi. I remember the "Chorus of the Hebrew Slaves."

(Quotes:)

"Oh, my country so lovely and lost" The theatre will now be the deportation center for all of the Jews in Amsterdam. We are being shipped to Germany. To work.

(Quotes:)

"Oh, remembrance so dear, so fraught with despair" Our creche is no longer a nursery. It is a holding place for those children deported with their parents. The Germans have retained the staff here. They need someone to help execute their plans.

[...]

I wanted to flee and go into hiding. But those children will need someone to be kind to them. They'll need someone who cares. So I will stay to help. I will stay for the children.

[...]

We play games and sing Dutch songs—sometimes Jewish—to pass the time.

(She sings a bit of the song—"The Little Red Hen.")

We do not speak of what goes on outside the windows. And across the street.

(To the children:)

"You must be good for your parents for when they come to take you back again. They are only gone for a short while. Soon you will be reunited."

(Beat.)

Sometimes there was no reunion, and the child would travel alone.

[…]

We are given a list of the children who will be leaving on transport. They file down the stairs, white with fear. They say nothing. It's as if they know what is happening. Out in the street, there is a brief, silent reunion with their parents. And then the trucks are loaded. The trams filled. And the grim journey begins. The nurses vow to be there when each child leaves our door. It will not heal our broken hearts—but it will help to calm the children. They look up at us as they go. Is that forgiveness in their eyes? Or condemning?

HONOR AND THE RIVER

Anton Dudley

Wawa doesn't like to speak to her son, Eliot, about the accidental drowning of his father. She has recently begun dating Alcestis Roberts, the coach of Eliot's boarding school rowing team. During practice one day, Eliot fell into the river and saw an image of his father; the event has forced them to speak.

WAWA. You asked me if I ever see your father. I didn't answer you at the time because...well, because I was afraid. I've never been with anyone else, Eliot—no, let me finish—your father was my first love and—losing him—I know a mother shouldn't say this to her son, but losing him: I thought I had nothing left. Not that I ever considered leaving you, but so much of who I am as a person I discovered with your father. I think it apt that no one knows my name: he named me Wawa. I tell people that my brothers came up with it, because it makes me look pathetic I think; I know it's not very modern to define yourself by your husband. Most people nowadays won't even take their husband's last name, let alone allow him to give a first. But it wasn't like that, not with him, we were each *other's* trophies and each other's lives. His only other life was the water and mine: this house. Both we made our homes. And those were our three passions: our homes, each other, and you.

[...]

Please, Eliot, let me speak, I know you feel I don't speak to you about things like this, but I was raised not to show weakness to one's children, I think a parent should always be a pillar of strength: something reliable and unbreakable. But I realize that strong, hard things are often not very comfortable. It is the soft things on which we lay our heads. And I never meant to close you out, Eliot, I just—the pain was too great—and I thought if I ignored it, I might move forward. And then Alcestis appeared and I didn't know what you would think. I didn't want to hurt you or make you think I was betraying your father, but—I get so lonely, Eliot... With you at school—and I know you should be there: your father wanted you there, and though you complain, I think it's right—I believe that in my heart or I wouldn't allow you to stay enrolled. But without my family here: this home, is only a house.

I like Alcestis, Eliot. He sees something in me. Something I thought had died along with your father. And I feel like a schoolgirl and I don't know how to act because it's new to me—and frightening. And yes, I do see your father. Sometimes. Sometimes when I am preparing to go out with Alcestis, I'll look in the mirror in our room and I'll see him, standing behind me in his swimsuit. Like that mirror is the surface of some body of water, and he's swimming just beneath it. But sometimes…sometimes he smiles at me, and I know it's all right. His smile fills me with courage and I know I can move on. And it's glorious. I feel as if I'm…floating. Does that sound strange?

IN DARFUR

Winter Miller

In the midst of the Darfur genocide, Hawa struggles to remember her past, before government militiamen raped her and killed her family.

HAWA. There is a myth—not mythical in the sense that it is false, but perhaps an exaggerated belief in the proverbs of African women. My mother had a favorite, I heard it ten thousand times: "You can't know at sunrise how this day will end, you can't know at sunset if the next day will come." It never meant anything to me until the day it did.

To remind myself I am still human inside, I repeat fragments of my former life over and over in my head. It is an exercise of dates, of memory, of survival. It goes like this: One year ago today I taught children in a schoolhouse in Karnoi. Two years ago I poured tea for Muhammed and nursed my son. Three years ago I studied for exams at university while Muhammed braided my hair. Four years ago I ate Ethiopian roti with Muhammed after class. Five years ago the same minus Muhammed. Six years ago I met city life in Khartoum. Seven years ago I dreamed of university and read Edith Wharton in the early mornings. Lily Bart. Lily Bart. Lily Bart. Lily Bart. Lily Bart. Lily Bart. How I loved Lily Bart.

IRENA'S VOW

Dan Gordon

Irena, now a woman in her late seventies, remembers for a group of American high school students the time she encountered the full horrors of the Holocaust as a young girl in Poland.

IRENA. And then, in the marketplace, while I was shopping for fresh produce for the Major, Rokita's soldiers sealed off the streets. They closed the shops. They ordered everyone out of sight...into their houses, their apartments. They tell them to close their shutters. But I hid. I watched from behind a fence. I watched them herd a mass of people...old people, small children, pregnant women, women with infants. They shoved them. They did beat them. They cursed at them. They did kick them. And then this woman pleads with Rokita who was there...he was the boss of the whole thing. "Please be careful of my baby." And Rokita says, "You're afraid the baby might get hurt? I can solve your problem. You won't have to be afraid anymore." And he grabs the baby from this poor, terrified woman, he holds it over his head, and he smashes the baby's brains out on the cobblestone and then he shoots the mother. And they did drive these poor people on through the streets into the woods. There were pits dug there. And I did see the mothers and fathers cover their children's eyes with their hands as they were shot. And I did see their bodies fall into the pits.

(IRENA *seems to watch it all again, in horror.)*

When it was all over, I come out of my hiding place to a clearing of freshly turned over earth, and I see what I think at first is a strange plant reaching up from the earth toward the sun. It is not a plant. It is a set of fingers poking up from the dirt from someone buried alive, someone still struggling to live. I run toward it and then I see the S.S. Sentries with their machines guns and I am too frightened to move. I am too frightened to do anything. I do nothing.

KNOW DOG

Kathryn Walat

In her former life Alice was a dog, running with the Huns and her canine soul mate, who is now reborn as Stanley, the loyal dog of Alice's neglectful husband Matthew. This woman-to-dog-to-man love triangle plays out in a hot and dusty backyard, with Stanley remaining just offstage, never quite revealing (to Alice's frustration) just how deep his canine memory runs. Here she stands next to a metal tub, which is filled with water. She holds a bottle of shampoo. She searches.

ALICE. I know you're still there. I don't see you, but see I've grown allergic to you—fluid is running through my head and so I know you're near. As if smelling you wasn't hard enough with this short nose. So get in the tub. Go on. This is no trick, Stanley, just a bath. Water. See. Splash splash. I don't bite. Not anymore. Not unless you want me to.

You've got fleas. I've got shampoo. Specially formulated for flea-bitten canines like yourself. I told Matthew his dog has fleas and what does he do. Hunts down shampoo. Scratches your ears. He holds your nose in his hands and looks into your eyes, Stanley, I saw that, those no-word words of understanding going between you—man to dog, dog to man—I was watching, I saw you look back.

I know you know what I'm saying. Yes I know you don't understand the words—I know exactly what it sounds like, the syllables, the tones, making patterns that your brain can't follow, can't grab on to until it gets to something like Stanley. Stanley. Staaaan-leeeee. But you know what I mean so don't play stupid dog, get in the tub.

(ALICE *steps into the tub.)*

Like this. In the water. You love the water. And it's the hottest day of the summer and here you are making me beg you in. Don't make me beg, dog.

(She splashes.)

I'll let you splash. I'll press the pads of your feet just the way you like it.
Stanley. Stanley. Stanley. Stanley. Come soak with me.
Why won't you come.
Am I—

Am I that—

(She sneezes. She sees STANLEY.*)*

Am I that odd. Inside this uncovered skin. There isn't a word for it, I know, but it keeps you standing over there. I won't touch you with my hands. I'll keep my fingers out of sight. Look I'll just put my head—my hair—next to your nose. Against the back of your neck.

(She lowers herself into the water.)

I still see fires at night when my eyes close, when they haze over while I'm watching television. When my hand touches water it touches a subterranean stream, Stanley.

I smell the same. You know that never changes. From one lifetime to the next.

*(*ALICE *looks at her hands. She holds them out to* STANLEY.*)*

See this. Look at this, Stanley. What does this mean.

THE LADIES

Anne Washburn

Eva Perón, Argentina's most famous first lady, meditates on suffering.

EVA. I have a terrifying affinity for suffering. Whenever I see suffering in one of my people I feel it also in my own body. I think that this is why I am afflicted with illnesses. People who are cold, who do not care for another person, they maintain their body at a cool regular temperature. Me, I have fevers—I love and I hate and I don't forget. I am like the people—they don't forget, they *can't* forget, they can't choose not to suffer. When you have power you can choose not to suffer. Who would not choose not to suffer? Suffering is difficult. One by one by one I see it, I see men rise up to the great heights, the air is rare up there, it is like wine, they become dizzy but they feel wonderful. They are like the deep sea divers who go down to the depths and there something happens to their blood, they become intoxicated, they can't think. They look at the weights on their feet and they think 'Why am I wearing weights on my feet? How silly is that?!' and they unbuckle themselves from the weights on their feet. And their bodies rush upwards through the water too fast, and their brains are crushed and when they arrive on the surface their bones are smashed and they float on the surface like a mangled limp thing. Like the vomit of whales which lies on top of the waves and is called ambergris and is an extremely expensive ingredient in the best perfume from Paris. That is what it is like at the heights; what is most rare, most costly and sought after is really just vomit. And they stand up there and they feel dizzy and they say what is this suffering that I am carrying around my neck. I feel so light and so wonderful and this suffering, the suffering of other people, is weighing me down, it is too heavy and too hot and so they release it, and they don't even watch it fall to the ground beneath them to see if it lands on anyone and hurts them. And then they feel terrific, they feel released. They feel like finally, they are what they always knew they were, deep down in their hearts. Now they are a figure in a fairy story. But they are too light. And at the heights the wind is very strong. Not long after that they lose their balance, and then they fall— falling, they gain a terrible weight. And their bodies lie on the ground in a bloody pulp. That is their fairy story.

THE LADIES

Anne Washburn

Imelda Marcos, politician and first lady of the Philippines, muses on her beauty and overcoming personal difficulties.

IMELDA. I think that there is an idea that people who are so very beautiful they are unmoved somehow by their own beauty but I assure you this isn't so. I look into a mirror and I take my own breath away. Vanity? Oh no. God made my face this way. He made it so that when people look at me they feel a catch in their chest, they are drawn to me. When I speak, they will listen to me; when I feel, they will feel with me.

Jesus said take this cup away from my lips. He said I don't want to drink from this anymore because the will of God—even Jesus felt this!—can be bitter. And there was a time, yes, early in my marriage when I said take this cup away from me. I don't want to drink any more. I would go into my bedroom and I would shut the door and I would climb onto my bed and I would kneel, on the coverlet, and I would hit my head, my beautiful beautiful head, that God gave me, I would hit it against the wall. *(She mimes driving her head forward.)* Over and over and over. I hit it into the wall, so many times, so hard, that I had dented the plaster, there was a kind of *(She raises her hand and pushes it forward against the air slightly to indicate.)* crater, in the plaster. And once I saw I had damaged the wall that was where I would aim my head. For that spot. And if I made another tiny crack, if I dented the plaster deeper, then I felt that I had accomplished something.

My husband took me to the States, to the NYU Medical Center and they did an examination and afterwards they took me aside. They said Imelda, you have to make a decision. Do you understand? I looked up and my eyes were full of tears. I said tell me what this decision is. They said you have to understand that this is the life your husband has chosen. If you want to live, you will have to leave him. Or. You will have to change.

And so I began every morning to say affirmations. I said "My life is beautiful" "I love my life." The men in the living room, very early in the morning or late at night, the dirty feet, the cigars and loud voices and bags of money, I said "This is all part of a higher, idealistic purpose." When my husband said to me 'Stand this way, no, this way, sing, you have to dress like this and go here and say this, not like that, like this, wave your arm that way, sing, didn't anyone ever teach you to think?? Sing, that isn't how you cut a ribbon, my God' I put aside my laziness and I said I will listen to him, and I will understand. "I believe in this, I will become this, I am going to be this, my life is beautiful. I love this life. I love my life."

And one morning I wake up, I go to the mirror, I look into my beautiful beautiful face and I say 'I love myself' and I realize, suddenly, I realize…that it is *true.*

I am like a butterfly who has shaken herself finally from the chrysalis. I go to the window and I spread my wings to dry in the sun. The world is so beautiful, I am so beautiful, there is so much that I can accomplish! And there are tears streaming down my cheeks. They are tears of joy.

I think that we are all so scared to embrace ourselves. We are so afraid, of what we can become.

LETTERS TO THE END OF THE WORLD

Anton Dudley

Tess lives an inconsequential life in New York City; her identical twin sister works with AIDS orphans in Zambia. They haven't spoken in years. Tess asks her friend Bryan to pretend to be her, so that she can pretend to be her sister—to say the words that Tess so desperately needs to hear.

TESS. I would sit like this. On some floor pillow in some African hotel. We'll say five star for now. I'm...slightly tired—yes, that's right, you've got it—I've just taken a direct flight across the Atlantic, but I still look gorgeous, because that's what I do. I'd sit there and wait. Patiently. And she'd come up to me. From working with her kids. Her hair would be up: like so. Her shirt always more buttoned up than mine: like so. Her voice, a little different from mine, not really in sound, but sort of in tone: something like this. And she'd stand here, in her stance, and she'd look at me. Deep into me. And she'd say, "Tess. You came. I'm so glad. You must have got my letter? I know, I'm sorry to send something so cagey: 'Tess. Come to Africa. I have something I have to tell you.' And then all that suspense. You must have been knitting yourself up the whole flight over. All the things that must've run through your head. We have such a history, Tess, you and I—there's really just too much to say—but—sister—I asked you to come here so I could tell you this: face to face. Tess... I love you." ...And that would be it. Those three words would be worth crossing the ocean to hear. She would kneel down on the floor, like so; look me deep in the eyes, like so; and she would say: "Tess...I love you."

[...]

I'd never ask for anything else as long as I live.

MARGINAL SAINTS

Lee Gundersheimer

Christina is a Hispanic high school student who was brought up Catholic but is a bit lapsed. She is worried that she is pregnant and does not know who to turn to. She has always felt an affinity with the statue of Saint Agnes—the patron saint of girls and, ironically, chastity—that sits in the courtyard of her local church and is praying in front of it for guidance. The monologue can be updated by substituting "Wheel of Fortune" and "show" for "One Life To Live" and "soap," and "Walking Dead" for "Buffy."

CHRISTINA. Oh, why the hell not. *(She kneels down to pray.)* Dear Saint Agnes, being that your area of expertise in the saint fields is those that screwed up along the way someplace or other, and since it looks like I probably have accomplished that big time, I guess that qualifies me to ask you for un poco de ayude and guidance here, if you're not too busy. *(Thunder is heard.)* I mean I know I'm not like even exactly worthy of your blessing, being as how I really probably never even believed in you really. I mean I know I'm being like this major opportunist just to even be down here praying to you, since most of the time I told people you didn't exist, I even wrote that in an essay in Sister Caterina's Third Grade English class, that my mother prays to saints, but I think she's nuts because I don't even believe they exist, but now—I'm really scared Saint Theresa. I'm scared enough to be sitting here hoping that I was so wrong, and that you are real and that you can help me because I've done something unforgivable. I mean definitely in yours and the holy churches eyes—but I'm not sure in mine. And that scares me even more, I mean the not knowing how I feel. I know I screwed up—sorry, made a mistake, but what I'm trying to say is I don't know exactly the size of the screw-up— Oh, perdóname, por favor. I don't mean to be disrespectful. I have a "garbage pail" for a mouth, ask mi mama. But you probably know that already, you probably know her on a first name basis as much as she prays to you—every morning, every night, and if it's bad enough, like when they laid off Papa, she'll pray a third time—mid-day just before her One Life To Live—which is some major devotion 'cause nothing is more important to her then that soap—not even Juanita and me. So like you're probably sick of talking to her, like I am with Rosanna Pinero, the perra with split-ends and dandruff sits in front of me in Geometry, that calls me like almost every night 'cause she's so lonely or something, 'cause I'm telling you no-one would listen to her but me, and I feel, I don't know, like sorry or whatever for her, so I will listen to her bitch on and on about how no guys ever even look at her, while I'm watching Buffy or something, but I'm not even really focusing on her, you know what I'm saying? I hope you aren't doing that with me. I hope if you are really even there to be listening to this, if you are real, as real as a saint can be—that you aren't like tuning into somebody else at the same time and not like given me your undeniable attention. Okay, let me get to the point. Like I said before, I may have done something awful, I mean I have done something awful. I had sex with my boyfriend Carlos. More than once. Twice. Just twice. And I know that is wrong, but I do love him, but I know it's still wrong, so I am sorry. I am. It's just I hope you'll forgive me enough for that to help me with the fact that I may have done something even worse. Please Saint Agnes, I will never doubt you ever again, I will absolutely one-hundred percent believe you are real, and spend the rest of my life praying to you like my mama prays to the Virgin—if you can just help me to please not be pregnant. It's been over two months now and I'm terrified. My best friend Consuela even went to get a test, I was so worried. Because...I feel different inside, Agnes, like something's growing... Please don't laugh at me like some of my friends have, and tell me I'm being a jerk. Freaking out for no good reason. I feel it. When I touch my belly here, it's like I can feel it's different. Please give me your help... *(She prays for a beat silently in Spanish.)* Would it be too much to ask for some sort of like little sign or something, just to let me know. Like those other saints, them Greek Orthodox ones, shed me a tear or something? Look at this you are covered in pigeon shit. Here let me clean you off. Shit, the least they can do is clean you off, give you a little bath now and then. Show you some respect.

MISS JULIE

adapted by Craig Lucas

FROM THE PLAY BY AUGUST STRINDBERG

While her father is away, the mistress of the house, Julie, toys with the affections and libido of her father's bootblack, Jean. Or is it Jean who toys with the mistress's affections and desire? The play takes apart the gender, class, and economic divides of its time and place, Sweden 1888. Because of what Julie reveals in this monologue, we see that the various ingredients that went into her conception are alive in her actions as well: a jumble of crossed boundaries and misunderstood power plays—men, women, rich, poor, wise, reckless. The play is Strindberg's answer to Ibsen's play, A Doll House.

MISS JULIE. You're just saying that... Plus, everybody knows my secrets. My mother, how common she was by birth. She was brought up to believe in equality for women, all that and...she thought marriage was just a prison, ownership, so...when my father proposed, she said she'd never marry him, but he could be her lover, that was fine. He said he couldn't see the woman he loved in any less of a position, a rank, than himself. She didn't care about any of that, respect, position, and he was so in love, he said yes. But by then he was shut off, shunned by everyone, friends, family; and he was always alone in the house, nothing else but her, he couldn't be satisfied with that. I was born, despite her best efforts to prevent it. So she decided to bring me up as "a child of nature," no rules or rank, I would learn everything a boy learns, I wouldn't subjugate myself to any man, I'd be an example to the world of how much a woman can accomplish on her own. I wore pants... Well, you saw, I learned how to take care of the horses, I had to groom and harness and learn farming and go hunting, skin the animals, and on the farm the men were put to women's tasks, were you here then? We almost went under, we were the laughing stock of everyone. Finally, my father must have woken up, put everything back to rights. My parents were married quietly in a private ceremony, my mother got sick, I don't know what it was, but she had pains all the time, hid herself in the attic, the garden; stayed out all night. Then there was the fire, I'm sure you heard. The house and stables everything, gone, and...there were suspicions of arson, because the accident happened right on the day after the new quarter began, the insurance premiums had been sent in, but…of course, the carelessness of a messenger… fate, delayed, by one day…so…

[…]

What does it matter? We were left with nothing. We stood on an empty hill and slept in the carriage. My father had no idea how to get the money to rebuild, he'd neglected everyone he knew. So my mother… sought advice from a brick manufacturer, a childhood friend, you know; my father borrowed, and he didn't have to pay interest! So strange. We rebuilt everything. *(Drinks more.)* Do you know who burned the estate?

THE MOST MASSIVE WOMAN WINS

Madeleine George

In the waiting room of a liposuction office, Sabine reveals her struggle to reconcile the half of her that is determined to shatter the glass ceiling with the half that wants to be accepted and desired.

SABINE. Like my friend Michael. Michael and I, we are best friends. We go for sushi and foxtrot once a month at the full moon. The thing is, all our conversations go like this: Michael tells me about his love life, I support him. Michael whines about his girlfriend, I console him. Michael moans about the horrors of latex, I sympathize, I hug him, I make him tea, and recently I have found myself possessed with rage absolutely every time I lay eyes on him. Because I am so very tired of being everyone's warm and fuzzy sounding board. I want to be a full-blown sexual threat right now. I want to get down on my hands and knees and do it, sweaty, hot, savage, wrong, morally rep-re-hensible... If my mother could hear me now...she wasn't out of her foundation garments long enough to have sex. I was an immaculate conception. My father stuck his tongue in her ear and bang, there I was, I appeared just like that on the kitchen counter in an attractive presentation basket. That's how we fat women do it, you know. We just close our eyes and think beautiful thoughts and our offspring arrive with the afternoon mail.

In undergrad psychology we learned about these people, they were called split-brain patients, and each hemisphere of their brain could work on a task without the other half knowing. In the films they showed us they taught this one guy to build blocks into towers with his left hand only. Then separately they taught his right hand to tear block towers down. On the last day of the experiment they let both the hands work together—the guy actually fought with himself in this film—his left hand tried to build a tower while his right hand constantly wrecked whatever he made. The hands started slapping each other and wrestling with the same block...

The one half of me, see, won't take no for an answer. This me's gonna go out there and take the corporate world by storm, if that's what I decide I want to do, or climb mountains, or pump gas, or write for TV, or…become a stock broker if I happen to feel like it. I do not need male approval to achieve my life goals. Like a fish needs a bicycle, and so on and so on.

But I just can't ignore my pathetic other side—it's so whiny and "needy" inside of me. I yearn for…human touch, God, it's embarrassing, sometimes all I want is to be looked at, admired, soothed and caressed. I still want the power, I still want to make money and go mountaineering. But the thing I want most right now, God, Santa, Gloria Steinem, is some person to love me and sleep in my bed.

First I hate myself for it, then I forgive myself lovingly, then I yell at myself for going soft on myself. Then I cry, usually, and then I get sullen and scowl. Stomp around the place dropping dishes and breaking bric-a-brac. Backlash! I scream, backlash, Sabine! You're contributing to the undeclared war against women! How could you! How dare you! You ought to be shot! Then I usually have a marshmallow sundae to calm myself down.

The saddest thing is, I've got no one to blame. God damn, I wrote my dissertation on this, I know the eight key symptoms and the ten warning signs and the twelve-step recovery program like the back of my hand. How can I be so smart and so stupid?

So I've made a very adult decision. If I can't change the world, I have to change myself. I'm gonna lay on my back and suck up the gas and fall into a deep sleep, and when the prince kisses me I'm gonna wake up and be beautiful. And then I'm gonna flush all my feminist morals down the can and I'm gonna sashay my butt out into the glittering suburban night and I'm gonna get laid, goddamnit. Like my mom used to say—you've made your cake, now you have to eat it. I hear you, Ma. Ain't it the truth.

THE MOST MASSIVE WOMAN WINS

Madeleine George

Through a series of photographs, Rennie reflects on growing up and her erratic relationship with her mother.

RENNIE. The first picture of me is at my first birthday party. In this one I am screaming with laughter and holding my hands up to show the camera that I am covered with chocolate cake. My face is smeared with it, it is all over the front of my pretty pink dress. Apparently I was quite verbally advanced, and my parents were showing me off when my uncle Jake said, Oh yeah? How smart is she? She's a genius, says my mother, she understands everything. Try it. She'll do anything you say.

So...Rennie, says my uncle Jake, smush that chocolate cake all over your face, sweetheart. Will you do that for me?

And I did it of course because I was just that smart and I ruined my dress and they took a picture of me humiliating myself when I was twelve months old.

(Flashbulb pops.)

This one is my mother's favorite. It's of her and me on one of our mother-daughter days, we're on the steps of the Met looking *very* close and what you don't see is Mother boring her knuckles into the small of my back saying Straighten up, sweetheart, it lengthens your neck. Now glow, come on, glow. We want this one to glow.

For awhile there is an absence of photos—when tummies are no longer little-girl cute. Mother hides me at family gatherings and I seem always to end up behind pieces of furniture. So we have no extant record of the long years of wanting, of wanting and wanting and being denied. Reaching for bread and peanut butter and having Slimfast thrust into my twelve-year-old fist. Mother says No, I am putting my foot down. She is putting her foot down, I see, and I see that to want and demand things is bad.

And when I finally want nothing, nothing at all, when I finally want so little I can barely get up in the morning, my head feels like a ten ton brick on my shoulders, my knees buckle walking from class to class, when I want so little the gentlest sounds scrape my ears and my skin is sore and my hair falls out, finally my mother pulls me out from behind the chaise longue and says This is my daughter Rennie! This is my wonderful, beautiful daughter. Out comes the camera!

(Flashbulb pops.)

The pictures reappear. All the while Mother says Sweetheart, you're beautiful. You really do glow.

(Flashbulb pops.)

In this one I am standing outside my own house, in a hideous dress I do not recall choosing, it is blue and it feels like a garbage bag next to my skin. I am wearing a floppy white orchid on my wrist and man, am I glowing. I am really fucking glowing. My smile is about this wide on my face though I don't know what I am smiling about because Andrew Marino has his hand on my back. We haven't even left the house yet, my mother is still snapping pictures and there he is, slinking his hand up my dress. Later we are in the dark and he is breathing so hard he is fogging the windshield and I say to him Andrew. No. No. And he says to me Rennie, you're beautiful. Please Rennie please, will you do it for me? I am saying, No, I am saying, Stop, but he does not hear me, I am not loud enough. I am so—*weak*. I am just…too…weak.

(Flashbulb pops.)

In this one my mother is getting remarried. She is a vision in indigo organdy, she looks half her age, her husband's in real estate. But heavens, where's Rennie? Rennie's not in this one. Rennie is wearing an attractive off-white linen pants suit, but she is not in her place at her mother's side because she is in the parish hall kitchen, devouring the three-foot-tall wedding cake meant to serve one hundred and eighty guests. It was just so pristine, floating there, with no one to guard it, no one to witness… I ate and I ate and I ate it all up until there wasn't one crumb left, not a single frosted rosette, and I held that whole cake inside my body, I had it all to myself. And then I threw it all up on the kitchen floor and I walked out the back door into the night.

THE MOST MASSIVE WOMAN WINS

Madeleine George

In the waiting room of a liposuction office, Cel recounts her lifelong battle with self-mutilation.

CEL. It starts with a girl maybe six maybe seven, looking down at herself seeing how—horrible she was! How gross like a monster. She didn't look anything like the other kids from 4-H, they were all skinny as rats from dragging goats through the mud and bending over fields in the blazing hot sun. In summer all kids' legs were scabby—but nobody had marks on them like I did, like Cel, Cel had some scars.

The first one came when I was six. I had split open my knee climbing through barbed wire and mama drove me to the hospital to get the thing stitched up with ugly dark thread, that's how deep it was. But I took those stitches out with scissors when I got home. I told my mama they came out in the bath but I could tell by the way she looked at me sidewise frying the eggs that she didn't believe it. All that summer I worked on my knee and by the time Labor Day rolled around my leg looked like it had been caught in a thresher, maybe.

After that she just seemed to find them, Cel, these cuts in her skin, these holes. They seemed to pop up without her even noticing. Some she put in there herself with the kitchen knives for killing the chickens or shears for the garden or the awl daddy used for punching holes in saddles.

Mama didn't know what to do with her girl. At first she didn't say anything, just folded her arms like so across her chest. What's happened to the backs of your feet she asked. You're picking those cuts of yours apart aren't you? What are you doing to yourself Celie? Why do you want to do such a thing to yourself? So she started buying extra boxes of Band-Aids and leaving them about the house in places she thought I might be likely to come across them. But I wanted to—take myself completely apart. I had dreams of my body parts spread out in the yard for everyone even the neighbors to see.

All the way through high school I did it at night when no one was looking. After my shower, when the skin was still soft. It was my thing to know. Then one day my husband found me on the floor of the bathroom, busted in without knocking… After that he kept watching me, keeping track where I went. I tried to lay still. I forgot things…left them to burn on the stove. My husband paced around and slammed the door on his way out. He accused me of letting the heat out in winter, letting animals in, stray cats and birds.

So I needed a final solution. Get rid of all of the flesh at once. I was poking a roaster chicken full of cloves getting ready for Sunday dinner and I went to light the broiler with a hard wooden match. Then it came to me. My body—I wanted to light it on fire. Hear the fat sizzle into smoke. With all the fat gone I could dance—more than that, I could run and jump and fly maybe even, just me and my bones running naked through the meadows feeling the breeze. It seemed so obvious—why hadn't I thought of this before? I struck one of the matches, stroked it smooth cross the rough edge of the box and I could feel the flame sparking and growing and swallowing the match head. I held it in front of my face. It flickered in my own breath. My thighs would go up first I thought then the rest of me would catch on quick. I lifted my leg and dropped the match onto my pants. For a moment—nothing, then—warm hot my leg started to jump—my skin was on fire! I screamed without meaning to Oh my God! I reeled around to face the counter my hands out in front of me reaching desperate—something, anything! Towel potholder glass of water… In my mind I heard Miss Moser from in front of the black board—stop, drop and roll, she said, if you ever catch fire just stop, drop and…

Later I went to the phone to call 911, shivering, numb. I caught fire, I said calmly into the phone. I was cooking a chicken. It escaped.

MY CALIFORNIA

Lisa D'Amour

California, 1927. Doreen, a San Francisco socialite, is well aware that her overbearing mother has sent her to the doctor with the hope that he will convince her to give up her unborn child. But Doreen has other plans.

DOREEN.
You ready, Doctor?
Analyze this.
Doreen Mary Baker
Saturday night, September something, 1927.

Dinner at Tracy's.

Fooping at
Snakey Jake's
Baby Boo's
Moon's
Maud's

Chantilly Meringue's (In Jack's roost)

The rent party at sha sha's

Then
Late night screech back at Jake's

Silver Dollar cakes at Jill's

Some shut eye at Jo Jo's
till the sun screamed its way
into the room…

And that was my Saturday night.

Your diagnosis, Sugarshack?

[…]

Momma says you're gonna read my dreams.
Straighten me out.

Well momma knows best, don't she?
Sitting round with her fancypants
talking poetry
politics
money
like she knows the difference between caviar and fish farts.

Then she runs her mouth hot to me
'bout spending my Grandma's money bone dry.

My Grandma left me money to do as I please.
And I know how to spend it:
On Pure Experience.

Pure Experience is all we got
that's gold, Doctor.

You know what that means?

It means
I'll romp stomp and bellyrub
till my prayerbones howl
and my dogs walk themselves
Foop
fa bop
Hoop
Swoop
shim sham shimmy shop

Fa bop
sha sha
Fa bop
sha sha sha
ZOOP!
Till your eyes
pop from their eyeholes
fall through the floor
and sprout into bushes of envy.

It's 1927 Doctor.
The world's a changing place.
And I ain't no dinosaur girl.

Don't try getting me to talk to Momma.
I've talked the talk to deaf ears long enough.
You know what she says?

Dancing dries up your pussywillow, young lady
Drinking sours your mothersmilk
Smoking turns ovaries to ashes.
And then young lady just where will you be?

Well.

(She puts her hand on her abdomen.)

If what my mother says is true
I will birth an ashen child.

That's right.
I take her out with me to
woop and wag and holler
when I stomp and hoot and wail
she is right there with me
My little ash girl.

What?
A Daddy?
She don't have no daddy.
This is a child of pure experience.
Shhhhhhhhh.

OEDIPUS

adapted by Ellen McLaughlin

FROM THE PLAY BY SOPHOCLES

Jocasta, Queen of Thebes, wife of the great King Oedipus, attempts to calm her husband's fears as he tries to unravel the truth about the murder of his predecessor, Jocasta's first husband. Oedipus has just been told by a soothsayer that he himself was the former king's murderer, the stranger he has just instigated a manhunt to find. She tells him of her long hatred of soothsayers and what they cost her in the past.

JOCASTA. But this means nothing.
Prophets and prophecies…they spawn nothing but mayhem and misery. I have learned this too well. The scars of that lesson still burn across my beating heart. It is prophecy I have to thank for my greatest sorrow, my deepest regret. I will tell you a story I have buried in memory. All the years of our happy life together, I couldn't bear to think of it. But I'll tell you now and let you judge for yourself the truth of prophecies. When I was first married to Laius, I had a child, a boy. He was born with open eyes and we stared at each other in amazement. He lay on me and I kissed his smooth feet, feet that had never touched earth. Three days I had him, that was all. On the third day, a vile prophecy was delivered to us. Not from God, you understand, just some old charlatan, jingling charms, but it was enough to wreak havoc. This child, this wide-eyed, wordless stranger I held in my arms, would be his father's murderer, the prophet said. The utter horror of it. Laius believed him. Panicked, he wrenched the baby from my breast and gave him over to the winter night to do its work. The last time I saw my child, he was curled naked in his father's arms, staring up at him in confusion, one tiny hand splayed above his father's thundering heart, as if to calm it. It was brute fear that killed that child. To trust that prophet was a terrible sin. No man can speak for the gods, no man can speak for the future. Nothing could be clearer—just look at what happened. For all his lethal caution, some group of men he never knew butchered Laius at a crossroads.

Fortune-tellers lie. And those who believe them are fools. Criminal stupidity. And I didn't have the strength to stop it. I let my child be taken from me, let them fling his life away on the bare rocks of Citheron as the winter night howled his tiny bones to ice. I have so little of him, just three days, nothing to remember. Only the glitter of his open eyes. When the nights are darkest, when the cold moves in, I feel the glint of them on me and I shudder for what he suffered, what I didn't save him from. My unlucky stranger. My king, why do you shiver?

PATTY RED PANTS

Trista Baldwin

When Patty Red Pants is unexpectedly reacquainted with her childhood friend Becky Bloom, old memories resurface. She rehashes an erotic and unsettling experience she had in the woods growing up.

PATTY RED PANTS. I'm standing at that place behind my house, that place on the edge of the woods, and I'm lookin' down there. Into the woods. I've never been. The woods aren't too thick in this part and I can see—there's no one there. And I just…well, I see a trail and I follow it. I'm in the woods now, and Oh. My. God! I can't believe this is just outside my house! I can't believe a place like this can be all dangerous—it's so pretty. I'm following the trail and—it looks like a camp-site: a circle of rocks and some burned stuff. Some, like, burned pictures of women—porno pictures. Matchbook, ripped label on a Budweiser bottle, this woman's pubic hair in the girlie magazine is, like, staring at me—some burnt old beer cans— Oh my God, I'm like, on sacred "guy ground." I wonder what the— I don't know—the boys—looking at these naked girls, how the boys talk, how their hair and their clothes and their hands— I hear a sound. Twig snaps? My heart jumps. I hold my breath. And I—I have no idea why—my hands are goin' up my shirt, they're shakin' like crazy, and I'm— I don't know why, but— I'm taking off my bra. It's a totally stupid bra, too, it's like a totally white, cross- your-heart, came-in-a-box, totally embarrassing bra, and I'm standin' there holdin' it in my hand, I'm lookin' around, and—and I—I don't know— I hang my bra on this tree—and I totally book.

[…]

…I go back into the woods—a couple of days later—I go back to that campsite—and I find my bra—in the dirt—with two holes burned into it—where my nipples would be.

Pluto Was a Planet

Laura Jacqmin

Cecilia, a Type-A Ivy League senior, has challenged Sabrina to have sex on tape as part of a secret society initiation challenge. When Sabrina turns the camera on Cecilia, her bravado quickly evaporates.

CECILIA. I don't know.

(Beat.)

I'm at a party.
I run into Abe.
I'm nervous. And I drink. A lot. I smoke. A lot. Even despite my asthma.
And I find myself in someone's room, alone, with him.
And he's got a little coke, which I don't really do, and I'm surprised he does, but he's like, do you want some? And I'm like, um, okay, I guess. And I don't really know how to do it because I never have before and he helps me.
He touches me—sort of smoothes this piece of hair away from my forehead because I'm sweating and my skin, it's sticky, or damp, rather, and your rational mind—in a situation like this—is going, how romantic can that possibly *be,* really, we're about to do *drugs* together, that's not sweet, that's not special, that's nothing, but still, despite all that, this *thrill* goes through me and I shiver, I actually shiver.
And I'm thinking, he's really fucked up.
And I'm sort of fucked up but I'm good enough to be able to pretend to be a lot fucked up, more than I usually am or usually get and therefore not afraid of making a fool of myself.
And I lean forward, and I'm about to kiss him and he closes his eyes and I lose the nerve to do this incredibly personal, intimate, thing.
So I unzip him instead.

[...]

And he opens his eyes and turns, sort of stumbles away from me. Like he's *embarrassed* for me. Like he's *ashamed* of what I want to *do* for him. With him.

And he leaves the room, he leaves me there, and when I come out a few minutes later, I say, where's Abe? And everyone says, he left.
He left.

(Beat.)

Because—all I'm saying, is—as a feminist or—I don't know, just as whatever—
What self-respecting guy, when he's fucked up, and you're fucked up—says no?

(Beat.)

And yes, I agree, as women we should *all* be seeking out the guy who carries you home and makes sure you get all the way up to the fourth floor of your dorm and into bed and shoes off and teeth brushed and on your side and not vomiting and who stays to make sure.
And doesn't touch. And doesn't ask. And *realizes* what is appropriate and what isn't.

(Beat.)

But why did he say no?
By turning away and running and not saying anything and pretending to have been so drunk or high or a combination of both that he doesn't remember?
Which he has to. Remember.
And who *doesn't* tell all his friends? That I'm such a slut. Who *doesn't* call a girl who does that sort of thing a slut?

(Beat.)

Why is it so hard?

(Beat.)

Do you have any Kleenex?

PO BOY TANGO

Kenneth Lin

Po Mama, a stern, but vivacious and loving matriarch, is making a cooking video for her estranged son, who left Taiwan for a new life in America, and has not been home since. This may be the last message she will ever get to him, and she passes down her most precious legacy.

PO MAMA. April Eighth. Seven a.m. Kaoshiung, Taiwan. Video number fifty-seven. A lesson for my son.

(She nods.)

Good morning, my son. Time for a new lesson. Before we begin, I want you to ask yourself, "How many hours did I sleep last night?" If it is not at least eight, you stop this tape immediately and close your eyes. Food is a gift from the gods. You have the honor of refining it. You must be responsible. You must be alert. And, I hope that you took my advice and ate something before you went to bed last night. Food before you fall asleep will make you dream and those dreams are what you must bring to your dish. Last night, I recommended a slice of orange peel under your tongue. <u>Sweet</u> dreams. Tonight you try a spoonful of salt. Yes. Do not wash it down with water. Tonight you sleep with salt in your mouth. So, good morning, my son, and welcome to Po Mama's Kitchen! This time we are really in Po Kitchen. I made lessons one to fifty-six from the studio. But, now that I am three quarters of a century old, I am beginning to see the wisdom of all the people who told me that my apartment is at the top of too many steps. "Taiwan has too many earthquakes!" I said, "No earthquake can topple Po Mama!" and I raced them up to the roof and looked at my view of the Pacific, breathing salt air while they were still panting on the second floor. But, sooner or later, the earthquake topples everyone. I came home from the hospital last night and my nurse had to carry me all the way to my bed.

(She holds up a pinkie.)

Skinny little thing from the Philippines. I say, "You're just a little thing!" She says, "I'm bigger than you." And oh, she was.

*(*PO MAMA *pats her cheeks.)*

Po Mama lost so much weight in the hospital. Doctors! From now on, I am going to drink a glass of milk every morning and do exercises, like this:

(She marches in place for a few moments and stops just before she is winded.)

I will be plump again in no time! It's a nice kitchen. You would like it. Look, you can see the ocean from this window. See? I have had this pepper plant since you and I were living in Taipei. Yes! Do you remember it? See how they grew? When the peppers fall, I give them to the little girls and they braid them into crowns. I tell them not to touch their eyes. Oh! I tell you now, just in case you need to know someday.

(She picks up a garbage can and lifts out the liner.)

This is where I keep all my jewelry. Thieves never look in your garbage! Of course you have to worry about someone throwing it away by accident, but that's why I've never had servants anyway. Now my nurse comes everyday, but I don't know how much she wants to use the garbage. If I change my spot, I will tell you. *(Beat.)* It is a nice kitchen. Maybe someday you will see it. Someday you will bring your family. Ha-ha. You know, when I was in the hospital, they wouldn't let me eat anything that had any taste and they took my blood every day. "For tests," they say. They took my blood out and they put the blood of a stranger back in. "To make me stronger," they say. Now that is just ridiculous. How do they know what they are putting back inside of me? They don't know what that person eats. How will they know it will make me strong? You want to make a person strong? You feed them the right things! If that is no use, The Sky is looking elsewhere and it's time to close one's eyes. Feeding a person blood with tubes or salt water with tubes! Ah! A person eats with his mouth, his tongue, his nose, his eyes! Your ear hears everything you chew! You feed from your arm and all you taste is the wound. Doctors! What do they know about the basics of things? Today, I show you real medicine. Today, my son, I teach you… broth!

REENTRY

Emily Ackerman and KJ Sanchez

Liz is a "liberal-leaning" New York artist. She has two brothers who are Marines. Though their lives couldn't be more different from hers, she tries desperately to understand and help them.

LIZ. Have you seen their tattoos? I have some of them on my phone. Here, let me show you.

[(Projection: a black band tattoo wrapping around a bicep.)]

This is John's. It's a mourning band. He said it hurt like hell to get it. And here, these are Charlie's…

[(Projection: a tattoo across the shoulder is a skeleton Grim Reaper wrapped in the American flag.)]

This is on one arm, and this is on the other…

[(Projection: A tattoo across the other shoulder of boots, an upside-down rifle, and helmet with the words "Brothers in Arms, never forgotten"—the memorial of a fallen Marine.)]

It says, "Brothers in arms, never forgotten."

(Pauses, then decides to continue:) A few weeks ago… Charlie had a flashback. It started with him not feeling right. He said that he wasn't feeling like himself. He was angry and couldn't control his emotions. And he did go to someone in his command. I don't know who—probably like a lower-ranking guy. And the guy was like, "Suck it up, you're a Marine." And I'm sure Charlie was like, "It's not a big deal. I lived." I'm making that up, but I feel that that's probably what happened. So he was back on the base and in a training op and he—you know, big loud noises, explosions…—and he had a flashback. He just froze. And that's a very big fucking deal when you're a Marine—when they're like "go, go, go" and you don't do anything—you just freeze.

[…]

And whoever it was, whatever douche told him to suck it up—it makes me furious, all this tough-guy, "PTSD is for pussies." I know, I know, it's not all like that—a lot of them do take it very seriously. Charlie's commanding officer did pull him out, and he's getting help. But Jesus, Charlie wouldn't even go to the doctor after the IED, when his eye was all fucked up…

[…]

The very same week Charlie gets taken out of the field? John fell apart… He was home alone, and he said he had been drinking by himself. And he drinks…he drinks a lot. And he was sitting out on his balcony, and he realized how exposed he was out there. You know, he saw all the positions where a sniper could be. He's sitting on his balcony in San Diego, California, and he's looking around for snipers. And he became absolutely convinced that someone was gonna come into his house and kill him. So he got his guns out. He had a shotgun pointed at the door. Thank God his roommate didn't come home. But he knew he was losing it. He knew it wasn't real. But it seemed and felt so real that he then knew that the only way to stop it…was to kill himself.

[…]

When they're deployed, you try not to think about it, but you do. You prepare yourself for the possibility—that they could get hurt, they could die. But you know…if they get hurt or whatever over there, well, at least it's the bad guy's fault. But if something happens *here?* Whose fault is that? I don't know what to do. I mean, really, what am I supposed to do? *(Gives up; can't talk anymore.)*

REENTRY

Emily Ackerman and KJ Sanchez

Suzanne comes from a military family and is the ex-wife of a Marine who has been deployed multiple times. She is optimistic and has an extraordinary, very dry sense of humor. She never feels sorry for herself or her family.

SUZANNE. Well, when they get back from Iraq, we have post-deployment briefs about what to expect. They get all the wives together. They are like, "Okay, when they come home, they are going to be jumpy. They are going to need time to adjust. Be careful about throwing a party. Maybe don't have too many people around at first. The noises kids make might upset them."

The first two times he came back, I understood it fine. I made sure I sent him a picture of my new haircut. I made sure the house looked the same as when he left, 'cause surprises are not a good thing when they come back. I would wake him up, you know, really gently. *(Demonstrates:)* "Jess, wake up…wake up." And I would make noises in my sleep so he would know I was there.

But one of the last times, I just wasn't thinking. And my father and uncle were both Marines—I come from a military family. So, this one night Jess had already gone to sleep, and I was up and messing around on the computer and I wanted to tell Jess something. And I went into the room and jumped on the bed and was like, "Jess! Jess!" And he turned and *(Demonstrates:)* —scchwwk—latched on to my neck. And started throttling me. And he's completely asleep. I'm like— *(Breathing hard.)* —and grabbing his arm and am like, "Baby please, please. It's me, it's me. Baby, I'm sorry." And he woke up and was like, "Omigod, I'm so sorry, I'm so sorry. Are you okay, are you okay?" And I'm like, "It's not your fault, it's not your fault. It's my fault. I forgot. I'm so sorry, baby. I'm so sorry." Like, I just forgot. I had been so detached from it this time, 'cause I had been through it so many times already and was like, "Whatever." It was definitely *interesting.*

No, we're not together now. Actually, our divorce was final a few months ago. A lot of reasons, but one of the main ones was that after he got back from his fourth deployment, he didn't want kids anymore.

Now, I catch a lot of shit from my friends for dating only military guys. But honestly, I don't know how to relate to other people. I mean, I spent seven years of the Marine Corps being my life. It was everything. And I was a good Marine Corps wife. I guess I just always knew that—I don't know—that I would marry someone who had been in the military. 'Cause I thought that it showed selflessness. Like, there is this guy that I work with, Mike. I'm like, "Dude, you are able-bodied. What the fuck are you doing? Why didn't you join the military? Why aren't you serving the country? You work at a bank—yay." I don't know...

SAND

Trista Baldwin

Kiesha, a young American soldier, is overseas guarding a gas station in the midst of a Middle Eastern desert. She befriends a fellow soldier and the two of them discuss how they ended up in their current circumstances.

KIESHA. You'll have to ask my recruiting officer, cuz I wouldn't have thought this up on my own. That's for damn sure.

None of my friends can believe it. I'm like the smiley quiet one in class.

But this one day, I was just feelin' real agitated. It's after school, I'm walking down the street, and there's this tattoo parlor, right? And I stop. I go in. And I look at these pictures, all these dragons and roses and I'm like, what would that do? So I walk out. And right there, is a recruiting office.

It's not like I could see some other picture of my future. I'd try. To get a picture in my mind. Like, when I'd be in bed, supposed to sleep, I'd go, *okay Kiesha think. You're gonna be graduatin' soon, whatcha gonna do whatcha wanna do.* I'd lay there squeezin' my brain, and no juice. The only pictures I'd get were these images of fallin'. Into the water, like… not screaming or slipping, not like a scary accident. Just falling. Still. Into such darkness…

I'm not talkin' any sense.

[…]

I guess I needed *something* to come along. I didn't think it was learnin' to kill people, but—

[…]

It all happened so fast, you know. I never thought I'd be in, like, a war. It don't feel real.

[…]

But it is.

SEVEN MINUTES IN HEAVEN

Steven Levenson

Six friends, all fourteen years old, play Seven Minutes in Heaven in Margot's basement as they wait to meet her cryptic boyfriend. Margot and Wade talk about their futures in the dark closet of her basement.

MARGOT. After college? Oh. We'll get married. It won't be a very big wedding. Just our family and our closest friends, on a beach somewhere. California maybe. My mom will cry the whole time. She'll be embarrassed afterwards when she looks at the pictures and her eyes are red and her make up is streaky. Mike will go to medical school and I'll go to law school. Afterwards Mike can start his own private practice. The worst part of his job will be telling a family bad news, and on days like that, he'll call me and I'll come home early and I'll hold him as tight as I can, and kiss him hard and say, look at me, Mike. Shh, Mike. Look at me. It's ok, Mike, you did everything you could do. I'll work at a firm just down the street from Mike's office, and some days, if we're not too busy, we'll meet up for lunch or a cup of coffee or just to say hi.

At night, we'll find little jars and fill them up with ten million fireflies. I'll hold my knees like this. Like I'm holding them right there. We'll go for a walk and he won't be late, and I'll act as normal as I can, and I'll wear his necklace until it breaks off and turns back into dirt and I won't say anything.

You'll have three kids.

[…]

Two of them will be yours, and then the last one you'll adopt. You'll name all of them after your favorite characters in your favorite books. You'll fill up jars with green apples and necklaces, and when you get old, you'll retire and put together all of your savings and buy a little cottage somewhere far away, where nothing else is, except for sheep and grass and the weather. You'll read books all day long and take walks for an hour on the last day, on Tuesday, the last day, and make fires in your fireplace and cook dinners from scratch and wait for your children and your grandchildren and your great-grandchildren to visit you. You'll have bony little fingers and the skin will hang off of your arms so you can see the blue veins underneath, like ropes.

I'll have age spots on my hands and Mike's eyesight won't bc great, and my arthritis will get worse, and then one morning, we won't wake up.

SLAG HEAP

Anton Dudley

Ashley and Dave were best friends, living on the street, in a forgotten post-industrial town. When Dave left her to pursue a glamorous life in London with his high school sweetheart, Fran, Ashley was left to fend for herself. Broken and hungry, she has traveled a long way to find him, but has found Fran in his London flat instead.

ASHLEY. You know that street, Fran? That bloody corner split between the pub and the paper shop and the public loo? An entire life can go right by unnoticed on that bloody corner. People pass it by at all hours. It's a corridor to most people, a pathway from somewhere to somewhere else. It was where I lived. I can tell you what each brick looks like, what it feels like. I know where all the stains are on the pavement, and I can tell you how the water will run into the sewer drains when the rain is too hard, as it often is. You give me a time of day and I'll tell you exactly where the shadows will be on the street, I've even interpreted the patterns they make. At five o'clock on a Summer day, the curved marquis from the hair dresser's shop casts its shadow into the one from the antennae on top of the pub—and in the middle of the road, directly under the wires of the traffic light, for exactly ten minutes you'll see what looks to be a rocking horse.

If you're a bit drunk or you've had an E, you'll see it move, it'll rock back and forth. And ten minutes you won't notice the world, you'll have forgotten the acid eating holes in your stomach and the itch on your scalp from not having a wash and the rip in your trousers where the air slaps your skin and the fear that the rain will drown you in your sleep, you'll drop all this and see a child—perhaps yourself—rocking away with no cares at all. And you'll forget that there's blokes who'll pay for a poke and that it really is the only way you can eat. And you'll forget that the one person who called you his friend got up and left, dropping fifty pounds on your head as you slept in the park and disappeared because some fucking twat who thinks with her cunt thought it might be nice to make a bloody connection with the only thing she could remember made her a person!

THE SPOON RIVER PROJECT

A PLAY WITH MUSIC

adapted by Tom Andolora

BASED ON *SPOON RIVER ANTHOLOGY* BY EDGAR LEE MASTERS

Georgine Sand Miner is a woman forced by fate to live her life on the fringes of society with great cunning. She attempts to set the record straight after Daniel M'Cumber describes their tumultuous relationship together to Mary McNeely.

GEORGINE SAND MINER.

A step-mother drove me from home, embittering me.
A squaw-man, a flaneur and dilettante, took my virtue.
For years I was his mistress—no one knew.
I learned from him the parasite cunning
With which I moved with the bluffs, like a flea on a dog.
All the time I was nothing but "very private," with different men.
Then Daniel, the radical, had me for years.
His sister called me his mistress;
And Daniel wrote me: "Shameful word, soiling our beautiful love!"
But my anger coiled, preparing its fangs.
My Lesbian friend next took a hand.
She hated Daniel's sister.
And Daniel despised her midget husband.
And she saw a chance for a poisonous thrust:
I must complain to the wife of Daniel's pursuit!
But before I did that I begged him to fly to London with me.
"Why not stay in the city just as we have?" he asked.
Then I turned submarine and revenged his repulse
In the arms of my dilettante friend. Then up to the surface,
Bearing the letter that Daniel wrote me

(She pulls the letter out from her garment.)

To prove my honor was all intact, showing it to his wife,
My Lesbian friend and everyone.
If Daniel had only shot me dead!
Instead of stripping me naked of lies,
A harlot in body and soul!

THE SPOON RIVER PROJECT

A PLAY WITH MUSIC

adapted by Tom Andolora

BASED ON *SPOON RIVER ANTHOLOGY* BY EDGAR LEE MASTERS

Elsa Wertman has held a secret her entire life. In this explosive monologue she is finally able to divulge this secret to the other residents of Spoon River.

ELSA WERTMAN. *(I would suggest she not use a German accent.)*
I was a peasant girl from Germany,
Blue-eyed, rosy, happy and strong.
And the first place I worked was at Thomas Greene's.
On a summer's day when she was away
He stole into the kitchen and took me
Right in his arms and kissed me on my throat,
I turning my head. Then neither of us
Seemed to know what happened.
And I cried for what would become of me.
And cried and cried as my secret began to show.
One day Mrs. Greene said she understood,
And would make no trouble for me,
And, being childless, would adopt it.
(He had given her a farm to be still.)
So she hid in the house and sent out rumors,
As if it were going to happen to her.
And all went well
and the child was born—
They were so kind to me.
Later I married Gus Wertman, and years passed.
But—at political rallies when sitters-by thought I was crying
At the eloquence of Hamilton Greene—
That was not it. No! I wanted to say:

(She indicates Hamilton Greene:) That's my son!

That's my son!

THE SPOON RIVER PROJECT

A PLAY WITH MUSIC

adapted by Tom Andolora

BASED ON *SPOON RIVER ANTHOLOGY* BY EDGAR LEE MASTERS

Zilpha Marsh, a school teacher in Spoon River, discovers a "gift" she has been given. This mystical gift both scares and delights her.

ZILPHA MARSH. *(As if she is telling a ghost story, which she is.)*
At four o'clock in late October
I sat alone in the country school-house
Back from the road 'mid stricken fields,
And an eddy of wind blew leaves on the pane,
And crooned in the flue of the cannon-stove,
With its open door blurring the shadows
With the spectral glow of a dying fire.
In an idle mood I was running the planchette—
All at once my wrist grew limp,
And my hand moved rapidly over the board,
Till the name of "Charles Guiteau" was spelled,
Who threatened to materialize before me.

(She screams out of fear and runs quickly stage right as she says:)

I rose and fled from the room bare-headed
Into the dusk, afraid of my gift.

(She is now stage right.)

And after that the spirits swarmed—
Chaucer, Caesar, Poe and Marlowe,
Cleopatra and Mrs. Surratt—
Wherever I went, with messages,—

(Using a voice of the naysayers of Spoon River:)

Mere trifling twaddle, Spoon River agreed.
You talk nonsense to children, don't you?

(Now in her own voice:)

And suppose I see what you never saw
And never heard of and have no word for,
I must talk nonsense when you ask me
What it is I see!

(She laughs maniacally and returns to her seat still laughing.)

STRETCH (A FANTASIA)

Susan Bernfield

Ohio, 2004. Rose Mary Woods, President Nixon's longtime secretary (who famously testified to mistakenly creating a gap in the Watergate tapes) is nearing the end of her life. In this fantasy flashback, a vigorous Rose makes a last great defense of her president.

ROSE. Mr. President, the wolves are at the door.
Mr. President, I'm not sure I can keep them out
anymore.
But I can keep it up, keep circling the wagons.
And I can keep a straight face.
And I can keep things running, keep a secret
keep whatever, whatever you need me to
you know I can as well as you know anything.

I have tried with my body and my brain
I have typed and stenoed and delegated
I have stretched
for Judge John Sirica and all the media
liberal and less so.
I have shown them my moves
how I reached for the phone
and my fingers slipped onto the wrong button
recording over your conversation, 4, 5 minutes at most
a terrible mistake I said in court, yet a simple one.
I have stretched
and I have heard the snickers from around the world
because I know that you—*you!*
I have seen you do the utmost good
I have seen good
good.

23 years of service, of respect.
18 ½ minutes of buzz.
Hum. Absence of conversation.
And nobody looks at me anymore

without asking a question.
Erasure.
For all my efforts, I have made the cover
of Time Magazine.
It was always a dream of mine—Secretary of the Year!

(Sound cue: tape buzz. She speaks faster, building in desperation and intensity.)

You and I know that secret is not always bad.
Inner circle, they spout that like an indictment.
But is anything more indicative of mutual trust?
Is anyone more without reproach
than the mutually trustworthy?
When you're in the position you're in
Mr. President
who should you want around you?
Strangers?
There are some protections
the Secret Service doesn't offer.

Mr. President, I have done my job.
You have dug yourself out of the doghouse before.
But this time it's wolves at the door.
They are nipping at our ankles
your ankles, you!
Who have done so much for our nation!
Done so much good for all of us!

(A last effort; convincing herself.)

I am telling everyone!
The President will never resign!

(Calmer; a new tack.)

And Jeane Dixon says
Jeane Dixon says that everything will turn out fine.
May will be a bad month, May and June, probably
but everything will turn out fine.
And isn't she the greatest psychic our
nation's ever seen? Isn't she the one who predicted
that God would make you great?

It makes me think—one of the first things I learned
when I moved to Washington.
When I transferred to your office, Mr. President,
when I became secretary to a Senator.

The floors are slippery in the
corridors of power.
Cold marble, cold and slick.

Don't wear your best heels.

THE SUMMER MOON

John Olive

The Summer Moon *follows the trials and adventures of Naotake Fukushima, a Japanese man who comes to California to sell (not very good) trucks. Naotake gets connected with Rosie, a shoot-from-the-hip Japanese American. In this monologue, Rosie waxes enthusiastic about the strawberry-growing land she's planning to buy.*

ROSIE. *(Pointing, excited:)* See this irrigation ditch? From the road, all the way back to that fence line, then down to the other ditch, then back to the road. Twenty acres. It's mine.

[...]

Well, it's not mine, not yet, I'm leasing it, from Johnny Nishimoto, I've worked for him a couple of times, he's semi-retiring. He says. Anyway, I can use the money I've made selling the trucks and then Johnny'll stake the balance after the berry harvest. That way I don't have to go to those thieving banks. He'll let me use his heavy tractor to disk and plow. If it works out, I can own this land in a year. It's good land. Lie down.

([...] ROSIE *points.)*

See how we're in sort of a bowl? That means the water'll run from both ditches into the center of the field. I can get berry beds through the whole field, I can do the whole twenty acres in strawberries. A lot of times it's hard to get the center of a field irrigated. Taste the soil.

(Holds out a handful.)

[...]

You don't have to eat it, just put your tongue on it, like this. Like this.

(Touches her tongue to a handful of soil. [...]*)*

Not alkaline at all. Beautiful sandy loam. Perfect. I ran into Johnny Nish in a café. Like magic. Magic magnetism. There's no such thing as coincidence. All you have to do is stand very still, and pretty soon you'll end up right where you're supposed to be. Trick is, you have to be *very relaxed.* I don't believe I'm doing this.

(Falls backward, onto the soil.)

I love this smell. It hangs in the air for days. The smell comes off the plants when you cut the berries, from the moistness of the roots, the softness of the soil. I love the California sun, it fills you up and makes you empty at the same time. Feel like I'm flying. [...]

TOPSY TURVY MOUSE

Peter Gil-Sheridan

Christine's daughter Sarah, a developmentally disabled young girl, was recently found floating in a nearby river, dead. Christine speaks at Sarah's funeral.

CHRISTINE. More than a few people encouraged me not to speak today. But I insisted. I have many reasons for standing before you but mostly, I wanted to speak because there wasn't anyone in this world who knew Sarah the way that I knew Sarah. Many people saw a girl with a handicap. She was a girl with a handicap. But of course I saw much much more. Mothers can see the truth of their children, if they take the time to really look. When Sarah was born, she looked like a perfectly normal baby. Before long though, I noticed that she never focused on anything. She just seemed to stare off into space…more than other babies do. I thought that maybe she was deaf, since she never seemed to notice loud bangs…or the vacuum cleaner. She didn't speak for the first time until she was four years old. She said "Chicken." Chicken! Can you imagine my relief?

Sarah grew up to be so much different than I expected her to be. You hear that your child has a developmental disability and you think, "What will she do? How will she have a life of her own? How will I?" This may surprise you some but she was quite independent. She served her own food. She bathed herself. She dressed herself. That explained the sea of purple. And I had expectations of her. I expected her to make her bed, to keep her things in order, sometimes I even asked her to make breakfast. Just cereal and milk and toast, really, but still, it was a respectable breakfast she could make on the days where I had to go to work earlier than usual. She still had her stuffed animals, her toys, but I figured that eventually she'd grow out of them and if she didn't, well what difference would that make? There are worse things in the world that an adult with a few toys. Much worse things.

Her favorite toy was her steering wheel toy that made her feel like she was driving because she couldn't wait to drive even though we all knew that she could never drive. We would always pretend. I'd say Sarah, "slow down, would you?" or "watch out for that fat guy on the bike." I was going to take her driving anyway, out to the country on a great big open field and let her do it for real someday because everyone should get the chance to be like everyone else. Everyone should have the chance to feel what it's like to be able to escape.

Sarah took great pride in her independence. Everyday she said, "Mom, I walked home from school, right?" Everyday she said, "Mom, I can take care of myself, right?" I would say yes and then I would remind her what to do in the case of an emergency. We went over it a thousand times! Sarah repeats a lot. Repeated. Repeats. Why didn't she do it? She must have been so afraid. I can't imagine how afraid she must have been. Oh Sarah, I should have locked you in the house and made you a world that was beautiful, a world that was safe. Won't you please forgive me? Won't you all please forgive me?

"I like to wear this dress to school because it's nice to wear a nice dress to school. Isn't it nice Mom? Can I take a bath? And wash my hair? I can't go to school without washing my hair. It's a nice dress. It's a nice dress. It's a nice dress."

Her voice was velvet to me.

I want to thank you all for what you've done for me in these last few days. I can't say that I ever wholly felt a part of this community. But now, in the midst of this tragedy, I have been surrounded by support, by an outpouring of love and compassion and for this, I thank God. I thank Him for the grace of my neighbors who mourn with me. Please come to see me. I'll be alone there. I'll keep a coffee cake on hand should any of you need a sweet and some coffee.

I'll think of you everyday, Sarah. Everyday until I turn to dust.

Thank you.

TROY WOMEN

adapted by Karen Hartman

FROM THE PLAY BY EURIPIDES

Helen has just learned that Menelaus, her estranged husband, means to execute her. She appeals to him.

HELEN. You have decided I'm the enemy
so you probably won't respond.
But I can guess how you'll accuse me
plus I have my own points to make.
I will balance the views.

You feel nothing, so let's use reason.
First, who caused this war?
Helen? Or Hecuba
who gave birth to Paris
the greedy guest?

Second, Priam sealed the doom of Troy
and me
when he refused to kill that son at birth
even though the prophets spelled out
this exact disaster.

And next?
Don't remember? I do.
Lucky Paris got to judge a beauty contest of goddesses.
They all tried to bribe him:
Hera said he could be king of Asia and Europe;
Athena promised triumph over Greece;
Aphrodite offered me.
Exquisite, she said,
unearthly,
complete.
Aphrodite won.
Who profited? Greece.
Unconquered.

While I became property.
Now you hate me
when you should crown me.
For I did more to keep Greece safe
than all the armies.
I gave my body
to keep Greece safe.

Look at me.

I know what you're thinking.
That's not the point.
Why did I go
Secretly, in night, with him?
Paris—did you name him, Queen Hecuba?
Paris came with the goddess to take me.
And you were gone, my one.
You were gone.
How could you?
How could you?

I must ask myself one private question:
What happened to my heart
to ever
ever
make me leave you,
my one?

Rage at Aphrodite
of infinite power
but forgive me.
Forgive me.

Look?

You might go on.
Once Paris died and no god cared for me
why didn't I come home?
You know what?
I tried.
I would climb the city walls
wind a rope around my body, tight,
tie this rope to a jutting stone

and lower myself—
bare toes searching out holds
rough rocks scraping my breasts—
towards the Greek camp.
The guards could tell you.
They caught me again and again.

Then there was a man who took what Troy didn't want.
Kept me in his house.
Raped me again and again.

Please look, Menelaus.
Yes.
Lover.
I have been stolen like a prize
kept like a beast.
I am human.

I know it isn't that kind of time but meeting your eyes I have to smile. Your face shows the rest of my life. I am starting to tremble, and you know me as a woman who often but not always keeps control.

The gods made me
and the war.
Do you hate them too?
You're smarter than that.
I know you.
I know you.

UNCLE VANYA

adapted by Craig Lucas

FROM THE PLAY BY ANTON CHEKHOV

Elena and her husband live off the estate run by Vanya and his niece, Sonya. Dr. Astrov, a frequent visitor to the estate, is the object of Sonya's desire, which she confides to Elena. Unfortunately, Elena is also smitten with Astrov. This speech occurs in Elena's first moments alone after Sonya has asked for Elena's advice and help in getting to Astrov.

ELENA. There's nothing worse than knowing someone's secret and not being able to help. He clearly doesn't love her, but why shouldn't he marry her? She's not pretty, but for a country doctor his age she'll make a great wife; she's intelligent, she's very kind…pure… No, that's not it… That's…

(Pause.)

I understand her misery. In the middle of desperate boredom, grey sky and vulgarity all around, no one even capable of anything other than eating, drinking and sleeping; he walks in, handsome, interesting, fascinating, like a bright clear moon rising in the dark… To lose oneself entirely in his charm… I guess I'm attracted too, a little. Certainly bored when he's not here. I smile thinking of him. Uncle Vanya says I have mermaid blood in my veins. "Let go at least once in your life." …Maybe I should. That's probably what I need… *(Looks directly in the eyes of the audience.)* Take off like a bird free of all their sleepy faces, their talk, and forget they all exist… But…I'm a coward, I'm shy… My conscience would torture me… He comes every day, I know why he's here and already I feel guilty, I should kneel in front of Sonya and apologize and weep…

VOICES IN CONFLICT

Bonnie Dickinson

Tammy Duckworth is an Iraq war veteran. She served as a U.S. Army helicopter pilot and suffered severe combat wounds, losing both of her legs and damaging her right arm. She was the first female double amputee of the Iraq War.

Tammy is a veterans' rights activist and in 2013 was elected as the U.S. Representative for Illinois' 8th congressional district. She is the first Asian-American woman elected to Congress in Illinois, the first disabled woman to be elected to the U.S. House of Representatives, and the first member of Congress born in Thailand.

MAJOR LADDA "TAMMY" DUCKWORTH. I am not going to dishonor the effort in saving my life by saying "woe is me I got no legs." Well I got one knee. There are guys who have none, guys who are blind. I have my arms, my face, my brain. This is a pretty good life I have compared to what it could be. Plus they make prosthetic high heels. I checked into it. Not three-inch stilettos, but at least an inch or two of heel. I'll be good to go.

I wanted a combat job not because I wanted to go into combat, but I didn't think it was fair. How could I be an equal soldier if I didn't take equal risk? At the time it was 1992, there was a lot of debate about allowing women in combat. In 1993, they finally let female aviators into combat.

What other country would let me do that? Not that many. I am a minority female who got to be a company commander. I like that I can serve my country.

I miss my body. I miss my strong, healthy body. I am addicted to America's Next Top Model. I love Tyra Banks. I think she's the greatest. I am addicted to that show. Sometimes I'm like, "I can't wear stilettos anymore." And then I go shopping, I have to compensate for how my legs look under clothes. But then those feelings go away.

We will have a party here at Walter Reed on my one-year anniversary—my alive day. It will be great. I am very blessed. I have a good employer, a good husband who has been here for me. I appreciate every day of my life.

The Woman Who Amuses Herself

Victor Lodato

Beth Tucker, an extremely shy third-grader, reads a homework assignment out loud: a report on Leonardo da Vinci's Mona Lisa. *Beth's thoughts on the subject give us a glimpse into her disturbing inner life.*

BETH TUCKER. "Who is the Woman in the Window?" By Beth Tucker. *(Pause.)* I used my beach towel to look at. I have a big beach towel with Mona Lisa's face on it. I hung it from my closet door. It's much bigger than the picture Miss Mattel gave us, and I could see it better at night without my glasses. The light from the supermarket across the street shines in my window and I could see her face if I woke up from a noise. Or just how you wake up in the middle of the night sometimes. Then I could look at her. But I didn't think of anything about her. I couldn't even make up the beginning of a story. I had seen her face a million times on my towel, but I couldn't come up with anything. It's like when you can't talk sometimes, and you feel sick in your stomach. Because you're supposed to say something and nothing comes out. *(Short pause.)* But then I had two dreams. Which is what I am putting as my story. I don't think this is cheating because these dreams came from my head. *(Short pause.)* There was the first dream which is this: A woman is dying in her bed. Her skin is all yellow like in the picture. She tries to say something but the words come out all in a cough. I put my ear up to her lips, and she says: "How do I look?" "Not too good," I tell her. When I say this, she starts laughing. I ask her what's so funny, and she says, "This is the end of the day." She says how tired she is and she closes her eyes. I shake her, but instead of waking her up, I wake up. *(Short pause.)* That was the first dream. The second dream is the one where I see the Mona Lisa sitting by the window with her hands crossed, just like she is in the painting. Except she is alive. And I am watching her, and she unfolds her arms and lifts them up, and then there are more arms, until I see she has eight, like a spider. Two of Mona Lisa's arms are holding little bells, and the arms are dancing, and the bells are ringing. In another hand, she has an apple, which she is eating. But the inside of the apple isn't white, it's red—and this makes her mouth red. Another arm is rubbing her belly. And then she has a hairbrush too, and she's brushing down her curly hair. Two of the arms lift over her head and take off the black veil—and they move the veil up and down in front of her face like she's playing peek-a-boo with a baby. *(Short pause.)* The last arm is dancing, too—but not like the ones with the bells. This last arm comes out toward you, and in the hand is a knife. The blade is bright, like it has a light inside it. I was afraid this was going to be one of my nightmares, but it wasn't. Even though she is like a monster from under the sea, she didn't scare me—because she is beautiful. *(Short pause.)* I just watch her for a long time—and then that's all I remember. I woke up in the morning and wrote down this story. *(She looks up at audience.)* That's all I remember.

THE WOODPECKER

Samuel Brett Williams

Arkadelphia, Arkansas. A trailer park. Martha writes a letter to her only child, Jimmy, who is at war.

MARTHA. Dear Jimmy, even though it's only been six months, it feels like ya've been gone, like, six million years. I miss ya' so much, but I know you're doing the Lord's will. Brother Eric prays for ya' every Sunday, and he told me when he had time—he wuz gonna write ya' a very, very encouragin' letter. So, ya' have that to look forward to. I know your Daddy hasn't been writin' ya', but that's just the way he is—ya' know? He's been workin' hard for new air conditioner. His little colored boy Maurice hasn't lost a fight yet. Your Daddy misses ya'—I can tell. He makes me set a plate for ya' at the dinner table every night—in honor of his little…well, ya' know he loves ya'.

(Beat.)

I ain't been doin' too much lately, but I have started singin' again. Whenever I'm ready—Brother Eric is gonna let me perform one Sunday—just like I used to. He's helping me practice every afternoon. Not only does he love God but he's a brilliant pianist as well. He remembers me—how I used to be.

(Beat.)

The other day I got a newspaper to look up garage sales, and I saw an article 'bout the Ivory-Billed Woodpecker. They call it the Great God Bird. Ain't that grand? Only thing is—people startin' to think it ain't real. They're offerin' a ten thousand dollar reward for "conclusive proof that it exists."

(Beat.)

I keep all the letters ya' send me. Put 'em on the refrigerator right below the Domino's coupons and right above the picture of your smile. Ya' gotta get home soon so ya' can show me the real thing. Ya' promised, remember? We both gotta keep our promises. 'Cuz it ain't a promise if ya' don't keep it. And everythin' good in the world is built on promises. I love ya'. Goodbye. Your Mamma.

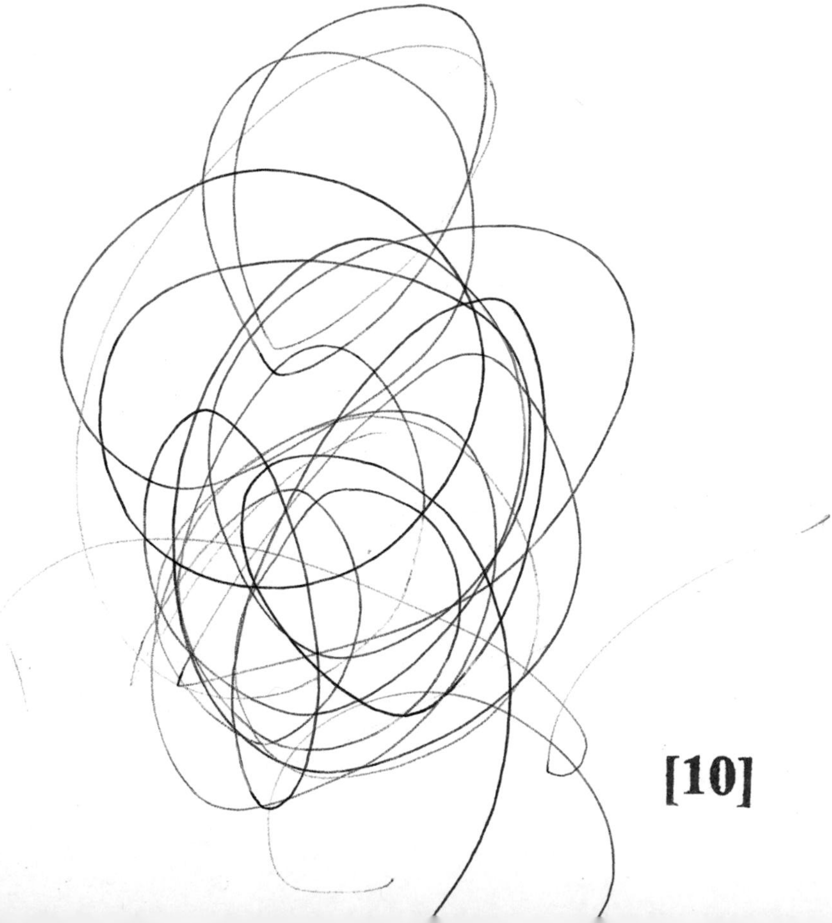

[10]